THE **WHARNCLIFFE**

COVENTRY

Hope you enjoy the book

best wishes

David McGrory

THE **WHARNCLIFFE COMPANION** TO

COVENTRY

AN **A** TO **Z** OF LOCAL HISTORY

DAVID MCGRORY

Wharncliffe Books

First published in Great Britain in 2008 by
Wharncliffe Local History
an imprint of
Pen & Sword Books Ltd
47 Church Street
Barnsley
South Yorkshire
S70 2AS

ISBN: 978-1-84563-048-5

A CIP catalogue record for this book is
available from the British Library

Typeset in 10/11.5pt Plantin by Pen & Sword Books
Printed and bound in England by CPI UK

Pen & Sword Books Ltd incorporates the imprints of
Pen & Sword Aviation, Pen & Sword Maritime, Pen & Sword Military,
Wharncliffe Books, Pen & Sword Select, Pen and Sword Military Classics
and *Leo Cooper.*

For a complete list of Pen & Sword titles, please contact
PEN & SWORD BOOKS LIMITED
47 Church Street, Barnsley, South Yorkshire, S70 2AS, England
E-mail: enquiries@pen-and-sword.co.uk
Website: www.pen-and-sword.co.uk

Contents

Introduction ix

Acknowledgements xi

**The Wharncliffe Companion to
Coventry: A–Z guide**

Aelfgar of Mercia 1

Arms 2

Auney, William de 3

Babbu Lacu 4

Bablake School 4

Barker, John 5

Barracks 6

Barrs Hill 7

Becks Riots 8

Bicycle (first) .9

Bishops of Coventry 11

Black Bull Inn 11

Black Death 13

Blitz 14

Bond's Hospital 15

Botoner 16

Bray, Charles .17

Brazil, Angela 17

Broadgate 18

Castle 18

Cemetery 21

Charterhouse .21

Cheylesmore Manor 23

Christchurch .24

City Wall 26

Coaches 31

Coinage 32

Cooper, Edward Ward 33

Corpus Christi Guild 35

Council House 35

County of Coventry 36

Coventry (the name) 36

Coventry Canal 38

Coventry Carol 39

Coventry Cross 39

Coventry Cups 42

Coventry Evening Telegraph 43

Coventry Priory 44

Coventry Tapestry 45

Cromwell, Oliver 48

Crow Moat 49

Cycles 50

Dickens, Charles 51

Dugdale, Sir William 52

Elections 52

Eliot, George .54

Farndon, Tom 56

Fire Service 56

Flying Wing 58

Football 58

Ford's Hospital 59

Forster, E M 61

Freemen 61

Gaol 62

Gee, David 63

Gill, Paddy 64

Godiva 65

Godiva Procession 68

Gosford Green 71

Great Flood 72

Guild Chair 74

Guilds 76

Hales, John 77

Harford, John 79

Harington, Sir John 79

Harris, Mary Dormer 80

Henry VI 81

Hewitt, John 83

Hinds 84

Hippodrome 85

Hob's Hole 86

Holland, Philemon 86

Holy Trinity Church 87

Horse Racing 89

Hospital of St John 91

Hutt, Arthur 92

Iron Age Village 93

Isabella, Queen 94

Jabet's Ash 95

Jaguar 96

Jopson's Coventry Mercury 97

Knave's Post 97

Lammas Riding 98

Langton, Walter 99

Leofric 100

Lord Mayor 101

Lunt 101

Martyrs 102

Mason, A E 104

Massey-Ferguson 104

Mill Dam 105

Motor Car 105

Mystery Plays 108

New House 110

Nod, Mount 111

Old Grammar School (St John's
    Hospital) 111

Osburga 113

Palace Yard 114

Parkes, Henry 117

Parkes, John 118

Peeping Tom 119

Phillips, John 120

Pilgrims 121

Police 122

Pool Meadow 124

Precinct 125

Prehistory 127

Prize Fighting 129

Quadrant 130
Radford Boulder 131
Radford War Memorial 131
Roman Remains 132
Rudge Cycles 134
Rupert, Prince 135
St George 135
St John The Baptist 138
St Mary's Hall 140
St Michael's (Old Cathedral) 143
St Michael's Cathedral 145
St Nicholas 146
Scots, Mary, Queen of 146
Seige of Coventry 147
Sent to Coventry 149
Shakespeare, William............151
Shelton, John Bailey 151
Sherbourne 152
Siddons, Sarah 153
Soldiers 154
Stocks 156

Stoddart, Andrew Ernest 158
Swanswell Pool 158
Swanswell Spring 159
Terry, Ellen 160
Thornton, John 161
Unions 161
Vauxhall.........................163
Watch Making 163
Water Supply 165
Watson, Samuel 167
Weaving 167
Wesley, John 169
White, Sir Thomas 169
Whitefriars 171
Whitefriars Gate 172
Whittle, Sir Frank 174
Wyken Pippin....................175
X Marks the Spot 175
Yugoslavia 175
Zulu 176

Introduction

Coventry is one of England's great historical towns and a companion such as this can only scratch the surface of its multi-faceted past and its rich characters. Although generally known as a modern town due to the rebuilding after the blitz, Coventry still manages to hold onto some of its past and visitors are often surprised by what remains. Not ancient streets, except Spon Street, but stunning buildings such as St Mary's Hall and Holy Trinity Church. For those who think Coventry is just cars, think again – for motor cars are just a small part of its extraordinary past, affecting only the past 100 odd years.

Over 1300 years ago St Osburga ruled over a house of nuns on the hillside of what we know as Broadgate Hill. History however does not start there, for in about 650 BC someone chose to bury two bronze axe heads, literally 15 feet from the present Godiva statue in Broadgate. Two axe heads tend not to be casual losses so the possibility arises that they may have been a ritual burial, making Broadgate an ancient ritual site. Recently a Roman ditch came to light at the bottom of Bayley Lane; Coventry's past continues to reach further back than anyone had previously suspected.

The earliest traveller to create an image of the city was William Smyth, Pursuivant Dragon to Elizabeth I, who drew a northern prospect of the walled city in 1576. The first to document a description of Coventry was probably John Taylor, the Water Poet, who visited the city in 1639 and wrote that Coventry was 'a faire, famous, sweet, and ancient city, so walled about with such strength and neatnesse as no city in England may compare with it'. This was praise indeed. In 1649 Wencelas Hollar engraved two prospects of the walled city from the north and south for Dugdale's great history of Warwickshire.

This great wall protected the city and made it an important Parliamentarian stronghold during the Civil War. Many flocked into the city at this time seeking its safety, but overcrowding began to cause problems and the council ordered the expulsion of many who didn't belong here or were considered undesirables. During the Commonwealth people who travelled in and out of the city on a Sunday did so at their own peril for in 1655 the mayor Robert Beake wrote in his diary, 'A soldier that came out of Scotland from travelling on the lord's day was put in the house of correction.' Beake also noted that three Quakers who travelled on a Sunday were put in the cage and suffered public humiliation, while others were set in the stocks. None could travel on the Lord's Day without special written permission.

By the end of the seventeenth century Coventry had a population of around 9,000. By 1748, with the introduction of new industries such as silk ribbon weaving, the population had risen to 12,177 and the city itself contained 2,065 houses. By the 1841 the population had reached 30,781, due to the continuing industrialization of the city, and many new houses were built within the grounds of existing buildings. The city was still unable to expand outwards at this time as the Lammas and Michaelmas Lands held by the Freemen had placed a collar around it. The exceptions to this were of course the 'New Towns' of Hillfields and Earlsdon which housed many weavers and watchmakers.

By 1888, with the birth of the cycle trade, Coventry's population had reached over 50,000 and the city was constituted a county borough. By 1911 the city also produced the motor car and to reflect this its population had grown massively to 106,377. Despite the growth in industry Coventry itself was noted as being a clean, healthy city. In 1937 it was written, 'By common consent, Birmingham had yesterday one of the most beautiful days of the early part of the year within living memory. But in Coventry the dust free atmosphere, for which the city of spires is justly famed, gave the day the tone of a Southern clime in early summer.' It appears that much of this was due to the fact that Coventry factories tended to be worked by electricity or gas. Coventry also had a very effective health system and in 1938 a public health committee was informed that Coventry was the healthiest place in the world. With this and the city riding high on motor car production its population continued to grow until it reached its peak in 1967, with a total of 335,238 people. Not surprisingly over the years, as the motor industry and many of its supply industries have disappeared, the population has gone into decline and presently numbers around 302,000.

Coventry has suffered much redevelopment from before the Second World War and, although some development is good, little has been learnt from past mistakes and as we enter the eighth year of the new millennium the boring 'box' building has began to make a return along with other out-of-scale modern buildings crowding out what few smaller scale older buildings we have left. Some of Coventry's ancient buildings are also sadly still classed as being at risk. Coventry itself is however thriving and continues into a bright future.

Acknowledgements

Many thanks to John Ashby, Jean Field, Roy Baron, Coventry Local Studies and Coventry's many historians of the past. Also for photos, John Ashby, Trevor Pring, Roy Baron, Cliff Barlow, Margaret Rylatt, Craig Taylor, Vic Terry, Tony Rose, West Midlands Police, Coventry City Libraries, Local Studies, *Coventry Evening Telegraph*, Coventry Transport Museum and CVOne. The rest of the photos are from the David McGrory Collection. Also a special thank you to Rob Orland for scanning the pictures used in this volume.

The Wharncliffe Companion to Coventry

A

AELFGAR OF MERCIA

Aelfgar was the sometimes wayward son of Earl Leofric and Lady Godiva. He was actively involved in a family feud between the Leofrics and the Godwins. When Aelfgar opposed the bestowal of Northumbria on Tostig Godwin, the brother of the future King Harold, he was outlawed, went to Ireland and went 'Viking'. Afterwards he joined King Griffith of North Wales and harried the Marches, so much so that Harold Godwin, the real power behind King Edward the Confessor, offered him a pardon to bring him back into line. The pardon was accepted and an uneasy alliance restored between the houses. Earl Leofric rode with Harold and brought his son's former ally under submission.

In 1057 Leofric died and Aelfgar became earl of Mercia. He succeeded to Leofric's land from the Wash to the Dee, but was not given Anglia, which went to Harold Godwin's brother Gyrth. This caused much resentment and the following year Aelfgar and Harold Godwin quarrelled again and Aelfgar was outlawed. He went back to Ireland and returned with a Galloglass army of Hebridean/Viking warriors. He also rejoined to his alliance with King Griffith and gave his daughter Ealdgyth in marriage to the king. Harold again offered the troublesome lord peace and again Aelfgar came back into line. In 1059 Harold tried to cement his alliance with the house of Leofric by marrying the now widowed Ealdgyth. Aelfgar did not however survive to see his daughter marry the king of England for he died in 1062 and was buried with great pomp in the church of St Mary in Coventry, by his illustrious father Leofric.

Edwin succeeded his father as earl of Mercia and his brother Morcar continued as a lord. In 1066 Harold Hardrada landed in Northumbria but was driven out by an army led by Edwin and Morcar. Earl Tostig Godwin joined Hardrada and defeated Edwin and Morcar. Meanwhile William landed at Hastings and King Harold took on and defeated the Viking army at Stamford Bridge. The English army then marched south, hoping to be joined by Edwin and Morcar's armies, but they were too late (it has been suggested deliberately because of the Leofric/Godwin family feud). Harold Godwinson and the English army were defeated at Hastings. London declared for the last

Edward the Confessor with two Saxon lords.

of Alfred's house, Eadgar the Aetheling, and Edwin and Morcar professed loyalty. However, when William's army reached Berkhamstead, they deserted the cause and sued for peace. Edwin and Morcar afterwards were allowed to keep their titles, but when William was out of England they backed an insurrection against him. On William's return they submitted to him and were pardoned.

ARMS

A coat of arms for the city first appears in the 1200s: with a split shield, one side red for Coventry, the other green for Lichfield, showing the joint diocese. In the shield was an elephant with a castle on its back. This is a double symbol of strength; the elephant being the strongest beast in the world which can bear the weight of a castle on its back. The earliest seal of the city has a tree behind the elephant, which comes from the medieval belief that elephants had no knees so they slept leaning against trees. Also of course the oak tree was yet another symbol of strength and steadfastness. On top of the shield was a cat o' mountain, a wild cat. It is said the cat was a symbol of watchfulness as, like lions, they were believed to sleep with their eyes open, hence ever watchful. Below was the motto, 'Camera Principis', which in the past has been said to have derived from Edward the Black Prince, who held Cheylesmore and was said to be a regular visitor to the city. The problem with this is that Edward was hardly ever in Coventry, except when he stayed at Cheylesmore Manor on his way to his grandmother's funeral. In fact the term could actually mean the chamber of the prince, as in the city of princes, royalty, kings and Coventry's close connection to many of them. This term was directly used towards Henry VI in a greeting in the fifteenth century.

In 1888 a closed helm was added above the shield, representing a borough, and in 1959 supporters were granted, the black eagle of Earl Leofric and the phoenix representing the city rising from the ashes of war.

AUNEY, WILLIAM DE

In the twelfth century Hugh Keviloc, earl of Chester and master of Coventry Castle, promised to do service on crusade in the Holy Land. Finding himself unable to keep his promise Hugh sent in his stead his man, William de Auney, being a knight in his service and his friend. William was said to be a man of great honour and also a valiant knight, proving his worth time after time. Before he returned home William contracted leprosy, the most feared disease in the medieval world. He returned to England but would not call on his lord for fear of infecting him. Earl Hugh was greatly distressed that his friend had caught leprosy in his service and swore to look after him, building him a house some distance outside of Coventry in an area which became known as Chapelfields.

Here William de Auney spent his last days. After his death Hugh extended the house and turned it into a leper hospital, adding to it a chapel dedicated to St Mary Magdalene, 'for the maintenance of such lepers as should happen to be in Coventry'. The chapel was served by a priest and brothers and sisters who cared for those who suffered from the fearsome malady. Later, as leprosy grew more common, the hospital was further extended and a second chapel was built on the site dedicated to St Leonard. This was to be used by the men, while the women attended St Mary's. The chapels and hospital were later acquired by Coventry Priory and later in the reign of Edward IV it came into possession of the king who passed it on to the canons of Studley. The house came to an end in Henry VIII's Dissolution and the buildings were converted into outbuildings and barns. Over the centuries, through lack of maintenance, the buildings gradually fell into total disrepair and eventually collapsed and were overgrown. In 1847 land on the junction of Allesley Old Road and Hearsall Lane was being cleared for building and the bases of the chapels came back into view, lying amid a scattering of half-buried broken statues of saints. These were cleared and built over, along with the memories of Earl Hugh's friend William de Auney.

B

BABBU LACU

The Babbu Lacu is the ancient name of the lake which once filled the lower levels between Barrs Hill and Broadgate Hill. This lake was fed by the Radford Brook and the Sherbourne and a number of other water sources. The lake originally stretched from beyond Pool Meadow to beyond Queen Victoria Road. It also stretched down the present Market Way and across to what is now the Swanswell. It is possible that the lake was also seasonal and grew in size during the wetter periods of the year. Its narrowest point was believed to measure some 200 yards, stretching from the present site of Bishop Street to the Burges.

The lake may have taken its name from the Celtic water and war goddess 'Badb' pronounced 'Bab'. She was known as the 'Washer at the ford' for it is said the goddess washed the blood-stained armour of the gods. Interestingly, Badb was also known as the 'Scald Crow' and on the northern side of the lake names such as 'Crow Moat', Crow Lane and Crow Mill survived until the early twentieth century.

One of the largest surviving remnants of the Babbu Lacu appears to be the Swanswell and long-gone St Osburg's Pool. Areas of water, like wells, which carried pagan associations were often Christianized by the church and that may be why the surviving section of the Babbu Lacu was renamed St Osburg's Pool after the local saint. The fact that a small Roman statue of Mars was found near the lake's narrowest crossing point and on the other side of the crossing another warrior, possibly again Mars, was found, suggests Mars's association with healing waters and as god of agriculture. Interestingly, the name of the other surviving remnant, the Swanswell (or Swineswell as it was originally known) may have ancient origins for it is said that the pool was formed by a giant boar ripping up the ground. This boar was said to have been dispatched by Sir Guy of Warwick. Celtic legend is full of stories of magical destructive giant boars that are killed by heroes after a destructive rampage. These animals were symbols of agricultural fertility and war gods like Mars. This could suggest an ancient origin to the pool or even may have been the legend behind the creation of the original great lake, the Babbu Lacu.

☛ *See* **ST JOHN THE BAPTIST**

BABLAKE SCHOOL

Tradition states that onetime mayor of Coventry Thomas Wheatley sent an agent to Spain to obtain steel wedges and when the wedges arrived in

Coventry they were actually silver. With this good fortune it has always been said that Wheatley founded Bablake School in 1560. In reality the school already existed but he did leave a bequest to it which from 1566 brought in the annual sum of £49. It is recorded that in 1507 Thomas Bond added his hospital onto the already established school and John Bedull is recorded as the school's master in 1522. The children of Bablake were from a poorer background than those at the grammar school and would receive free board and education for two years before being apprenticed to a master.

Bablake School in Hill Street.

BARKER, JOHN

John Barker was deputy lieutenant or governor of Coventry during the first Civil War. Barker, a draper, lived in Cross Cheaping and was mayor of Coventry in 1634. He became Member of Parliament in 1640 and deputy lieutenant in 1642. He was made mayor for the second time in 1644 and as a strict Presbyterian rendered good service to the Parliamentarian cause as long as his party led. It is said that Barker always appeared in public wearing a military buff coat and carrying his sword. On the passing of the Self

Denying Ordinance in 1645 the Presbyterians fell from power and Barker resigned from his post and as commander of a regiment of foot. When the Long Parliament was purged in 1648, to clear those who opposed the King's trial, 150 Presbyterians were ejected, including Barker, who it is said was forcibly removed from the house. This event caused quite a stir in the city and soldiers had to be sent to keep the peace.

After the purge Barker fell on bad times and in 1661 appealed for assistance from the city corporation. He had spent hundreds for the good of the city and once in 1642 had offered to pay £1,000 for its defence. In 1670 Barker, now aged 79 years, was in dire straits and made his final plea to the corporation to save him from starvation, which thankfully they did.

BARRACKS

Before Coventry had a barracks it was a garrison city, taking in hundreds of troops on regular occasions. In May 1756 we are informed that 126 licensed victuallers took in over 600 troops. The Rose and Crown, which still exists in the High Street as the Courtyard, took in fourteen soldiers while the now-gone King's Head in Smithford Street was reserved for ten officers. In 1772 the 4th Regiment of Dragoons was billeted in the city. During this stay a Corporal Jackson, staying at the Unicorn by Coventry Cross, fatally wounded a civilian with his hanger and was put on trial. In 1777 the 6th Inniskillen Regiment of Dragoons were billeted in the city after returning from Scotland. In 1793, with the threat from France, the ancient Bull's Head Inn and its huge yard known as the Bull Yard was purchased by the government and made into an army barracks. This initially housed Dragoons; in the latter part of 1801 two troops of the 1st Dragoon Guards occupied the barracks. They were replaced in September by seven troops of blue-uniformed Royal Horse Guards. In April 1830 the 5th Regiment of the Dragoon Guards occupied the barracks and celebrated the king's birthday here by firing volleys in Broadgate while the band played 'God Save the King'. In October the same year the 60th King's Own Royal Rifles stayed as they passed through to Carlisle. While here two soldiers were court-martialled and received 300 lashes.

In April 1834 the barracks housed the 3rd Dragoons, who were waiting to be replaced by the 8th Hussars; the city soon after was made headquarters of the Dragoons. During their period in the city the regiment also maintained a band which played in the Barrack Square on a Sunday when it was open to the public. The band also accompanied the troops to church and played while the officers dined in the evening. This was greatly enjoyed by some citizens of Coventry, although not by the Revd Sibree of Vicar Lane (which lay by the barracks) who complained about the noise interfering with his services. Later the regiment was moved to Birmingham. From the mid-nineteenth century

Coventry Barracks photographed in the 1880s during the Royal Artillery's occupation.

the barracks became the home for many years to regiments of the Royal Artillery. From 1908 to 1914 the barracks became the base of the Warwickshire Royal Horse Artillery, who left the barracks for the last time on the outbreak of the First World War. Coventry Barracks was closed in 1922 and was soon turned into the Barrack's Market. In the twentieth century most of its site became the Barracks Car Park.

☞ *See* **BLACK BULL INN**

BARRS HILL

Barrs Hill is a large area of raised land on the northern side of Coventry city centre, running towards the centre and away towards Radford. This area was described by Sir William Dugdale in the seventeenth century as being the most ancient part of the city, 'without the Bishop-gate'. Its name is actually derived from the Celtic word 'barr', meaning hill top. It is suspected that the hill top may have been the home to a bronze or Iron Age hill fort as formerly it had defensive ditches cut into it. Part of this area has been excavated and numerous cattle remains were unearthed. In a deed granted to Isabell Kyrvyne in 1577 it is referred to as 'Medelborowe ways leading from

Coventre to Radeforde'. The word Medelborowe comes from an ancient word used to describe ancient fortifications. The name survives today as Middleborough Road.

Until the mid-nineteenth century a prehistoric hollow way survived, leading down the hillside to the Radford Brook. The ancient sunken track was wide enough for one man to walk down without being seen and is a common feature in many prehistoric hill forts. The hollow way was filled up in the late nineteenth century. Part of this lane may have been connected with an ancient track way which crossed the hill top from east to west called 'Lideat Lane'. That name means the 'covered path', suggesting this too was an ancient hollow way.

Local tradition says that the Roman general Agricola built a camp on Barrs Hill and named the nearby settlement after the Roman water goddess, 'Coventina'. Agricola certainly did pass through this area as he marched north. Barrs Hill in the past has turned up Roman pottery and coins from the first to fourth centuries, matching the period covered by the Lunt Fort at Baginton.

From aerial photographs it is possible to see a large possible round barrow site on the northern side of the hill top and along Lydgate Road a row of house platforms of later seventeenth-century squatters' cottages.

BECK RIOTS

On 7 November 1831 the ribbon out-weavers of Coventry were in a militant mood, as their masters were giving them out-work at a very reduced price. This caused much hardship and anger in the city and at the beginning of November a meeting was called in a large hall in Little Park Street. At this meeting a committee was appointed to gather information on the masters who had reduced out-weaving prices and to find out about by how much they had been reduced. The meeting broke up and resumed later with a crowd of about 300 in Cross Cheaping. During this second meeting agitated weavers were goaded by others who brought to their attention that a nearby manufactory was using steam-powered looms and such looms would one day see them all in the workhouse.

A mob of about 400 to 500 broke off from the meeting and headed for Josiah Beck's factory in Beck's Yard, backing onto the River Sherbourne off the upper part of New Buildings. The mob banged on Beck's gate and he came out to ask them what they wanted. They wanted to see the power looms and Beck agreed to let a few in to see them. As they walked in, the whole mob surged forward into the yard, knocking Beck to the ground. They then threatened his life to get Beck to order his servant to open the factory door. The mob rushed inside and started to smash up the building, then continued upstairs where the looms were destroyed. The factory, which actually consisted of a dwelling house and weaving shop, was then set ablaze and fire soon ripped through the floors, engulfing the entire building. Beck desperately struggled to escape the mob that began to stone him; he was pushed around on a cart and escaped a second time only to be caught again later by the Mill Dam. Here Beck was put on his knees and his life was threatened and it seemed that some of the mob were close to actually killing him, had not Thomas Burbury stopped them.

The Riot Act was read and soldiers from the 14th Light Dragoon and 7th Hussars rode from the Barracks to restore order. The city's most respectable citizens were sworn in as constables and order was finally restored. By midnight all was quiet. During the hours of darkness William Westwick, Joseph Day and Benjamin Sparkes were arrested and in the morning Alfred Toogood, Thomas Burbury and John Deeming were also taken. On 17 November the men were committed to trial. Deeming was found not guilty. Sparkes and Burbury were initially sentenced to death but their punishment was afterwards changed to transportation, along with the other offenders.

Soon after the men were transported there were calls for some of their sentences to be shortened, especially the life sentence of Thomas Burbury who was at the riot but was not seen to take part. Burbury had also stepped forward to save Beck under threat by the mob at the Mill Dam. A public subscription was raised to send Burbury's wife and child out to him. In January 1834 Burbury wrote an open letter to the people of Coventry and its MPs thanking them for their support in sending his family and trying to shorten his sentence. At the time he was at Ansty Barton in Van Dieman's Land, working as a shepherd tending 800 sheep for his master, who had 10,000 sheep and 40,000 acres. In 1876 it was reported that Alfred Toogood, who took an active part in the riot, was now a well-to-do and respectable man. As for Thomas Beck, the man who introduced the steam loom to Coventry, he died in October 1876 a poor inmate of Bablake Hospital. It was said that he had never recovered or prospered after the riot.

BICYCLE (FIRST)

The usual story about the origins of the cycle in Coventry is that in November 1868 Josiah Turner's nephew, Rowley Turner, brought back the first cycle from France, rode it through the streets causing a stir and thereafter James Starley and Josiah Turner built the first cycles at the Coventry Machinist Company. E W Cooper however, Starley's assistant, says that the cycle came to England without Turner and he himself rode it for the first time in the streets. Although it is generally accepted that this first machine was French, it could have originated locally for there is another who

An early cycle: the first safety cycle designed by Harry Lawson.

claims to have produced the first all-metal, spoked wheeled cycle. E L Fardon, a well-known and respected engineer and blacksmith from Stoneleigh, told the press in 1890 that he started work on the first spoked suspension wheel in autumn 1868 at his home, then in Kenilworth. The completed wheels with steel spokes and Indian rubber tyres were added to his iron framed cycle and he rode it to and around Coventry for six months, causing much interest, even having crowds gather around it in Broadgate.

At the time he states that wooden velocipedes were being made in Bridgewater and the manager of that company offered Fardon £25 for the rights to his wheel, but he refused. Fardon later sold his cycle for £20 to a French cook at Stoneleigh Abbey named Robandy. Fardon said, 'He rode it about for a long time then he went to Paris. Afterwards he wrote to someone in the neighbourhood saying . . . my velocipede was the best friend he had ever had'. Interestingly, the velocipede which took off in Paris was the same design as Fardon's machine. This French-made machine was sent to Coventry in March 1870 and the design kicked off the city's massive cycle industry.

☞ *See* **RUDGE CYCLES; EDWARD WARD COOPER**

BISHOPS OF COVENTRY

The see was removed from Chester to Coventry in 1102 with the consent of King Henry I and by authority of a bull from Pope Pascal I. There were six resident bishops of Coventry, Robert de Lymsey 1102, Robert Peche 1121, Roger de Clinton 1129, Walter Durdent 1149, Richard Peche 1161 and Gerard le Pucella 1183. Most of these bishops were enthroned in Coventry Cathedral. Lymsey, Peche, Durdent and le Pucella were all buried at Coventry. Roger de Clinton died while on Crusade in the Holy Land and Richard Peche was buried at Stafford. These bishops who all signed themselves 'Coventry Episcopi' held Coventry Priory from the crown for nearly a hundred years. After the see moved to Lichfield it continued for four and a half centuries as the See of Coventry and Lichfield until the Restoration. When Coventry Cathedral was taken by the crown the bishop was Rowland Lee. He had previously married Henry VIII to Ann Boleyn and was ordered to persuade Sir Thomas More (whose sister lived in Coventry) and Bishop Fisher to changes in the religion. Lee later thought his connection to the King might save Coventry's cathedral but his pleas fell on deaf ears.

The seal of Richard Peche, bishop of Coventry, 1161–82.

BLACK BULL INN

The Black Bull Inn in Smithford Street was the largest inn in Coventry and dated to at least the fifteenth century. Apart from the main building its massive yard, known as the Bull Yard, later housed Coventry Barracks. After his victory at Bosworth it is generally believed that Henry VII came to Coventry and stayed at the Black Bull, then the home of Robert Onley. While there he watched from its window Thomas Harrington, a captured Yorkist, being beheaded on the conduit opposite. The city annals claim that Harrington called himself the son of the duke of Clarence, but that claim belonged to another: Lambert Simnel. However, one version of the city annals states that the King stayed at Onley's house which was 'against the Bull Conduit' – that would place it on the opposite side of the road. Another source says he stayed at the mayor's house, 'adjoining the Bull Inn'. This would place it back across the road again, but not in the Bull.

Another notable visitor who definitely stayed at the Bull in November 1569 was Mary Queen of Scots who was brought to Coventry because of a feared plot in the north. She came with the earls of Shrewsbury and Huntingdon and 500 men. Mary was put up in the Bull with her fifty

The Black Bull Inn *in Smithford Street.*

servants, taking over the entire building. The Queen was informed that Huntingdon and Shrewsbury could get no room at the inn and were concerned that the Queen's 'people' had too easy access to her. Elizabeth wrote back chastizing them for putting the Scottish Queen in a 'common inn'. She suggested Coventry Castle, which was ruinous at the time, or Whitefriars where she herself stayed. Whitefriars wasn't available initially but a week later Mary was removed from the 'common inn' to spend a day and a night in the Old Mayoress's Parlour in St Mary's Hall before being placed within the walled confines of Whitefriars.

During the year 1605 the inn was said to have been the meeting place of some of the Gunpowder Plotters: they met here just before the attempted abduction of the Princess Elizabeth from Coombe Abbey. Later that century in 1642 the earl of Northampton came into the inn seeking like-minded individuals to support the King and take the city in his name. As Charles marched with an army to the city, Northampton got little support and in fear of his life fled through the back door of the inn, riding out through the Bull Yard. The Black Bull Inn was sold to the crown and in 1793 converted in a new barracks for the city.

☞ *See* **ST MARY'S HALL**

BLACK DEATH
In 1349 the city had a visitation of the Black Death and the city annals say: 'A great pestilence happened in this citty, and throughout the realme, the living scarcely sufficed to bury the dead.' Another source states that, when the churchyards were full, the bodies were taken and buried in the fields. One victim of this visitation was Henry le Spicer, a wealthy spice merchant who owned a number of properties in the city. The year 1361 saw another visitation to Coventry and its surrounds for Robert de Stoke, lord of the manor of Stoke, was one of its early victims. It returned again late in 1364 and continued into the following year. During this visitation a number of priests died in Coventry and the pope himself authorized Prior William Greneburgh to ordain a number of younger 22-year-old monks as priests to try to replace them. One version of the city annals claims that in 1478 in the city and liberties 4,450 people died of the plague.

The visitations continue, for in 1564 we are told the 'death' took 224 souls. In 1574 plague again hit the city and thirty died within Bond's Hospital. One old man was said to have accompanied the body of his daughter to the grave in St Michael's churchyard, then at the end of the service fell down dead himself; three hours later he joined her in the grave. Other visitations continued on and off until the end of the century. During a visitation in 1579 the Common Council ordered that four men be appointed weekly to bury the dead. The men were to be paid 4 shillings each and were to reside separately from everyone else in a barn in Hill Street.

In 1604 the city had another visitation and 494 Coventrians died of the plague and £300 was raised to treat the sick. The city annals claim that during this visitation all the inhabitants of St John's Street were wiped out and were buried in a hollow by the city wall next to the footpath leading from New Gate to the Park. Thereafter St John's Street was known as Dead Lane. During a later visitation in 1625–6 to avoid infection many left the confines of the city wall and built temporary houses in Greyfriars (Sheriff's) Orchard (site of the Quadrant) and down in Cheylesmore Park by Quinton Pool. The registers of Holy Trinity church give telling evidence of this epidemic. On 7 October they record the death from plague of 'A Childe of Ridlies in Welstreet'. This is followed on the 10th with 'A Childe of Ridlies in Welstreet', then on the 21st, 'An other childe of Ridlies'. Then on 26 October, 'An other childe of Ridlies', followed the next day with 'Ridley himselfe buried'. After this visitation some made permanent arrangements and acquired second homes outside the city for just such occasions. From 1630, alderman and mercer Henry Smyth, his son Matthew and his wife leased a cottage and land, including a rabbit warren, in Canley from Coventry skinner Thomas Towers so they could flee there when 'there is plague in Coventry'.

In June 1665, because of the fear of plague being brought from London, the Corporation ordered that a constant guard be kept at the city gates between 6 am and 9 pm. From July, as the threat increased, no person known to be from London was allowed to enter the city and those already in the city were turned out on pain of imprisonment. The watch was increased to twenty-four hours and Coventry survived unscathed while London lost over 68,000 citizens.

BLITZ

Air raid shelters first began to be dug on Greyfriars Green in 1938, a whole year before the Second World War started. When the war did begin gas masks were issued to all citizens and all the emergency services were quickly created. Soon family air raid shelters began to be issued around the city, mainly Anderson shelters which were half buried in the back gardens. Evacuation was talked about but few could see the point as Coventry was so far inland. Limited evacuation did however take place. Coventry's factories went into overdrive with war production, aeroplanes, munitions and military vehicles trundled off the production lines and a huge temporary workforce moved into the city, lodging and living in temporary hostels.

The first local raid took place on 25 June 1940 when bombs were dropped on Ansty Aerodrome. The first heavy raid on Coventry itself was on 25 August 1940 when the almost new Rex Cinema in Corporation Street was destroyed. Regular minor raids continued and on 8 November the RAF bombed Munich using Coventry-built Whitley bombers. Hitler ordered a massive attack on Coventry and on the evening of 14 November 1940 around 500 bombers headed for Coventry and unloaded, over an eleven-hour period, 500 tons of high explosives, 30,000 incendiary bombs and 50 land and oil mines. Stan Morris recalls that night in the Radford area:

> *A stick of bombs ripped up the junction of Moseley Avenue and Lawrence Saunders Road. It was as if a giant can opener had ripped open the ground. You could have got three double decker buses in a line in that hole . . . Barker Butts School was wrecked by an aerial torpedo that ran along the ground and exploded. Some houses and shops at the corner of Three Spires Avenue and Christchurch Road were destroyed by a land mine and the smell of gas was terrible. A lot of shops were wrecked or completely demolished. The Co-op on the corner of Moseley Avenue was just a heap of rubble with burning food and exploding tins. It had been hit by an oil bomb and the smell was very unpleasant.*

My own father spent that night digging out those trapped under the rubble that had previously been the church of St Nicholas, Radford. In Cramper's Field the following morning the dead lay under a black tarpaulin on the

The morning of 15 November 1940 and Hertford Street still burns.

green. Over the previous night 554 were killed and 865 injured. The centre of the city had received hours of bombing and was devastated. The Germans coined a new word for this devastation, 'Coventrated'.

Minor raids continued and on the 8 April 1941 the city sustained a heavy eight-hour raid. The bombers returned again on the 10th and bombed the city for six hours. Over the war the city was bombed on forty-one separate occasions, leaving 1,200 dead. The last bomber to pass over the city was in August 1942.

BOND'S HOSPITAL

In 1507 the ex-mayor of Coventry Thomas Bond founded Bond's Hospital in Hill Street. It was built for the reception of ten 'poor men and one poor woman to prepare their meat and drink'. Bond's will stipulated that every inmate was to wear a hooded black gown and attend nearby St John's church for matins, mass and evensong and to pray daily with the priest for the souls of the hospital's founder, Thomas Bond, his father and grandfather and for the souls of all Christians. The inmates were chosen by members of the Trinity Guild whose souls the inmates also prayed for. Bond's will gave land

Bond's Hospital in its shared courtyard with Bablake School on the right.

and tenements in various parts of the city and in Leicester to maintain the hospital and to give alms to the poor. When the Trinity Guild was suppressed in 1547 the lands of the hospital were confiscated, but they were later returned by the council who continued the good work. Bond's Hospital is still used for its original purpose and has in recent years been extended.

BOTONER

Botoners were a family of wealthy merchants associated with the building of St Michael's church. William and Adam Botoner were both three times mayors of Coventry and gave £100 a year for twenty-two years to build the tower of the church. There was once a brass plaque in St Michael's which read, 'William and Adam built the tower, Ann and Mary built the spire; William and Adam built the church, Ann and Mary built the quire.' This came from an old rhyme and is probably an exaggeration: Ann and Mary Botoner could not have built the choir and the spire as there was a sixty-year gap between each construction.

BRAY, CHARLES

Charles Bray was perhaps Coventry's best known ribbon manufacturer, not particularly for ribbons but for his association with novelist Mary Ann Evans, alias George Eliot. Bray and his wife Cara lived at Rosehill, a nineteenth-century villa which stood between the Radford Road and St Nicholas Street on the site of the present Coventry Coachmaker's Club. Rosehill was a magnet, as Bray put it, to all crackpots who came through Coventry. These crackpots included of course George Eliot, William Makepeace Thackeray (who wrote part of the *Newcomes* at Rosehill) and numerous other writers, politicians and notables. Bray was a political animal and a free-thinker. It was Charles and Cara and her sister, Sarah Hennell, who most influenced Mary Ann's life and encouraged her to write. Bray published her first writings in his *Coventry Herald* newspaper.

An engraving of Charles Bray at the age of 73 years.

BRAZIL, ANGELA

Angela Brazil, the 'schoolgirl's friend', was born in Preston, Lancs, in 1868 and was educated in a private college in Manchester. After the death of her husband she travelled extensively and spent several winters living in Sicily and Italy with her daughters. Her first book, *A Terrible Tomboy*, was followed by *The Fortunes of Phillippa*, which was in fact an account of her mother's early life. In 1911 she moved to the Quadrant with her elder sister Amy and her elder brother Dr Walter Brazil. Angela had many other interests, including history, music, nature and painting, at which she was very proficient. In Coventry in 1932 she was asked about her writing:

> *Inspiration comes to me in a flash . . . then I think and think and think until the whole plot is mapped out . . . I even sort out the chapters mentally and give them titles. I imagine the characters, visualise their actions, and almost hear them speak. Then I start to write. In my early days I used to write and burn, write and burn again, but by now I have steadied myself down until my original work hardly needs any revision . . .*

Angela Brazil wrote forty-five schoolgirl novels, which were translated in many other languages. She constantly received letters and pictures from young girls around the world which she proudly kept in her study in the Quadrant. Here she would sit in a large armchair before the fire with notepad and pencil and write her books. Her summers, however, were mainly spent in her bungalow in Polperro in Cornwall. Angela Brazil's love of history was reflected in the fact that she was secretary of the Coventry City Guild which established Coventry's first museum in Bablake School. She died on 12 March 1947 after a stroll up Hertford Street.

BROADGATE

Broadgate, which stands on top of a hill, anciently may have been a site of some significance as in around 650 BC two Bronze Age axe heads were buried here. There was ancient track running through which was also used by the Romans, as coins found here testify. In the twelfth century Broadgate acquired its name, for here was the 'latam portum' or the 'broad gate' mentioned in Hugh Keviloc's deed which also refers to Coventry Castle. Since those early days when markets would be held around the castle gates, Broadgate has been the heart of Coventry, being a meeting place and marketplace through most of its days.

There have been many changes over the centuries, with its buildings being timbered, then brick, then concrete and steel. Old Broadgate was destroyed in 1940 and a new Broadgate was built around an island, home to the Godiva statue. In the 1970s one side of the island disappeared and later still, around 1990, half of the site was built on with Cathedral Lanes Shopping Mall. The 1990s also saw the erection in Broadgate of the 'tent', a much hated structure covering much of what remained.

C

CASTLE

The original Coventry Castle appears to have been a motte and bailey type with wooden tower and enclosure. The motte would have been between the Golden Cross and Broadgate and the bailey followed the line of Hay Lane, Bailey Lane and Earl Street. This castle was most likely built around 1139 during the Barons' War by Ranulf Gernon, earl of Chester, a 'consummate warrior, glittering with arms'. In 1143 this castle was put under siege by Sir Robert Marmion of Tamworth. Marmion at this time was on Gernon's side but it appears that Gernon had previously promised him the castle and wasn't true to his word, so Marmion came to take it. Marmion threw the monks out of the monastery and fortified it and dug man traps in the land between the hill top and the castle. While sitting it out Marmion got into the habit of riding out before the castle, goading Gernon to respond. One particular day the gates opened and Gernon's men rode forth, followed by foot soldiers. Marmion, alone, was suddenly in a panic and galloped back to the monastery. His hurry was however so great that he accidentally rode into one of his own traps, was trapped under his horse and decapitated by a common foot soldier.

In 1145 Gernon was imprisoned by King Stephen who ordered him to surrender all his castles. King Stephen then acquired Coventry Castle himself. The following year Gernon was released and put up a temporary siege castle against Coventry Castle. Gesta Stephani, written shortly after the event, says:

> *Also in front of the castle of Coventry, whither the King's men had withdrawn, the earl himself fortified a castle and valorously checked their sorties over the country until the King arrived escorted by a fine and numerous body of knights, gave the garrison fresh supplies . . . and fought a number of engagements with the earl . . .*

Gernon had laid ambushes for the King on the way to the castle and the 'deeds' record that when they met in Coventry there were heavy casualties, even the King himself was wounded and had to retire to the castle to recover. When Stephen regained his strength he led another attack against Gernon and this time put him to flight, nearly killing him. Stephen then lay against the earl's siege castle and eventually took it and razed it to the ground. Ranulf Gernon was poisoned and died in December 1153.

Shortly after this it appears that Coventry Castle was rebuilt in stone, with the motte removed and buildings set within a square enclosure. This castle is mentioned in the 1160 charter of Gernon's son Hugh Keviloc who mentions the 'Broadgate of my castle'. In 1172 Hugh joined Robert of Leicester in a rebellion against Henry II. Henry sent a force into the Midlands led by Richard de Lucy who put Coventry Castle under siege. Hugh lost Coventry in 1173 but regained it in 1179. He died in 1181 and his interest in Coventry was inherited by his son Ranulf Blundeville. In a charter around 1199–1204 of the nationally famed Earl Ranulf Blundeville, the castle is mentioned for the last time when he forbids his constables to bring burghers to the castle to plead for causes. It appears from this time the castle was run down and gradually sold off.

In the mid-twelfth century the Langley Cartulary refers to the church of St Michael, the earl's church, 'in ballivo', in the bailey. The same source for 1144–6 records a grant to Eustace fitz John of property near the 'south gate'. As there was no city wall at this time, this can only refer to the south gate of the castle. Interestingly Eustace was made constable of Chester Castle, so was he also constable of Coventry Castle? Dover Castle has a Constables Gate which was the castle constable's residence.

Coventry Castle was probably already in ruins in 1215 when King John ordered the slighting of a number of castles. As he held Kenilworth, Coventry

A stylized battle outside a twelfth-century castle.

was expendable, so it was sold off. In the 1220s a grant was made from Elias Despenser to Walter, son of Terry of Coventry, of the bake house called the Castle Bake house, *furnu castelli*. Around the same period or slightly later a grant was made by Roger le Gardiner of his 'entire garden' called the 'Earls Garden' around the site of the castle. The 'garden' had formally belonged to William Deyvallo. In the 1230s William Gran and others were imprisoned in Roger de Montalt's prison, which is likely to have been in the remains of the castle. The men escaped into nearby St Michael's church. In 1262 we find in the Eyre Rolls an interesting entry for Broadgate to a deceased tenant who formerly lived there: his name, taken from the place he lived, was Herman Attcastelgate. In 1293–7 a grant of Alice Stevechchale of land in Earl Street extends 'towards the south up to the castle ditch, fossatum castelli'.

All the remains of the castle are around St Mary's Hall and the hall itself appears to be made from stone originally taken from quarries north and south of Coventry, then robbed from the castle ruins. Large stone blocks also appear out of context high up in the building as if they have been removed from lower sections of ruins which still stood at the rear of the hall in the late 1500s. Caesars Tower at the rear bears a name only found on castle towers. It was originally three-storeyed with battlements. The battlements received considerable restoration in 1470 and 1473. The low doorway is for defensive purposes and was mentioned in 1395. Caesars Tower is exactly in line with the castle entrance and is actually wedged shaped. If the tower was mirrored it would have created a narrowing entrance for defensive purposes, with a wooden walkway above for the murder holes. The original tower when excavated in 1900 was believed to date from the twelfth century and its stones were cut with an adze. It also had sockets in the side of the tower to support the wooden beams joining the two towers and creating the walkway above. Beyond this tower outside the keep was the castle bake house – outside the keep because of the fire risk. Beyond this Hay Lane marks the first ditch, then an 18 foot V trench, then a third ditch at the entrance at the top of Broadgate. It was next to this entrance in the early 1200s that Herman Attcastelgate lived, by Coventry's long-lost castle.

CEMETERY

Coventry's main parish cemeteries were around the large but shared churchyards of Holy Trinity and St Michael. In the past graves had been emptied and reused, as the charnel house under the Marler's Chapel, on the north side of Holy Trinity, bears witness. Trinity had an extension added to its churchyard on the north side in 1776. This was excavated in 1999/2000 as part of the Phoenix Initiative and around 4,000 remains were removed and reburied. Part of the cemetery of St Michael was built over in the nineteenth century with Victorian buildings, such as the Triumph works in Priory Street. A further large area of the churchyard disappeared in the early 1950s with the building of Coventry University, then the Lanchester Polytechnic.

Under a Public Health Act of 1844 the Council acquired part of Whitley Common which had at one time served as a quarry for a new cemetery. The London Road Cemetery was designed by Coventry MP Joseph Paxton, the designer of the Crystal Palace. In its beautiful landscaped ground two chapels were constructed, one Church of England the other Nonconformist, and when Paxton died in 1844 a monument was erected to him at the entrance. Paxton's new cemetery was described in its time as being more like a gentlemen's park than a city of the dead. The cemetery holds monuments to many notable figures, such as George Eliot's friends Charles and Cara Bray, Coventry's national prize fighter Paddy Gill, James Starley the father of the cycle industry and many more. It also contains the mass burial of those who were killed in Coventry's blitz.

CHARTERHOUSE

The Charterhouse stands in an old area known as Shortley and takes its name from the French, 'Chartreuse'. This Carthusian house was dedicated to St Anne and started by Lord Zouch of Harringworth who gave land to the

Charterhouse as it appeared in the 1960s. Almost all of the windows are of a later date. Also note the blocked in medieval doorway under the later chimney breast.

brothers with the agreement of Sir Baldwin Freville. Later it emerged that neither of these men actually had any right to give away the land. This led to many legal battles until it was acquired by John Langley in 1417. Langley's coat of arms appears on a pennant carried by Longinus in a wall painting which still partially survives in the building. On 6 September 1385 Richard II and his Queen Anne had laid the foundation stone of the building. Richard showed particular interest in this house (dedicated to his queen's patron saint) giving it more land than any other. Coventry's notable Botoner family who gave so much to the construction of St Michael's contributed to the construction of choir, church and cloisters of St Anne's church. They also gave money to build the friars' accommodation. Each friar had their own small cell-like building, one up, one down, overlooking a square walled courtyard. The friars lived the lifestyle of a hermit and only gathered together for religious services and to eat. They were considered one of the strictest orders in the country, so much so that particularly awkward friars were sent here to be put in their place. This monastic house was after the Dissolution converted into a private house and the great hall is now separated into different rooms, including an upstairs, thus wall paintings can be seen starting on one floor and finishing on the next. An imperfect Latin inscription on one painting says, 'the house has been completed, and Prior Soland [1411–17] had a hard labour indeed in the building, and Thomas Lambard was procurator, putting away deceits'.

CHEYLESMORE MANOR

A large portion of the south of Coventry called the Manor of Cheylesmore originated with Leofric and Godiva, before passing into the hands of the earls of Chester, the last of whom was Ranulf Blundeville who died in 1232. The estate then passed on to the earl of Arundel through his marriage to Ranulf's sister Mabel. It is believed that around 1237 he built Cheylesmore manor house to replace the old castle in the centre of Coventry. In more settled times the moated manor house offered a more pleasant aspect overlooking open countryside. The manor then passed to the 5th earl who died in 1243, then on to Lord Roger de Montalt and his wife Cicely. In 1249 Roger and Cicely agreed to rent the manor of Cheylesmore to Coventry Priory for £107 a year. This did not however include the manor house and park.

The house and park remained with the Montalts and later Robert and

Cheylesmore Manor around 1900 showing the gatehouse and the surviving section of the manor house at the rear.

Emma Montalt agreed that, if Robert died, the manor would revert to Queen Isabella. This happened in 1330 and after her death it passed to her grandson, Edward of Woodstock, the Black Prince. When he died the manor passed to his son Richard II who had the city wall diverted to encompass the manor house. Cheylesmore Park at the time was said to cover 436 acres, consisting of pasture, woodland and moor, inhabited by deer and other game animals.

In the reign of Edward VI the manor was granted to John Dudley, earl of Warwick, who in turn leased the manor to the corporation on condition that eighty cows and twenty geldings belonging to the poor were allowed to graze here. In the seventeenth century the manor was returned to Charles I, but was then lost to the throne during the Commonwealth. At the Restoration the corporation gave it back to newly crowned King Charles II who snubbed them by leasing it to Sir Thomas Townsend. The latter lived at the manor house until 1685 then after his death the building was divided into separate tenements. The corporation obtained the lease in 1727 and in 1787 the lease was acquired by Lord Beauchamp from the prince of Wales. The following year it passed into the hands of William Preest, who turned the area nearest the city wall into allotments and enclosed part of the park itself. The royal connection ended in 1819 when the prince of Wales sold the estate to the marquis of Hertford and in 1871 it came into the hands of H W Eaton, Lord Cheylesmore. The land was thereafter gradually sold off and built upon.

The manor house itself was originally a stone-based timber-topped building with a large open courtyard, entered through a timbered gateway, and all was originally enclosed by a moat. Part of the original manor house was still standing in the 1940s as it had been converted into flats. Despite its historic importance and its 'magnificent roof timber' the remains of Cheylesmore manor house were demolished in 1955. The gate house however still survives and is currently the oldest Registry Office in England.

CHRISTCHURCH

In 1230 Ranulf Blundeville gave land on the outskirts of the town to a new order of friars called the Franciscans, founded by St Francis of Assisi. These grey-habited friars were sworn to poverty and walked barefoot, preaching the word outside their cloisters. Many saw the grey friars as a return to true religious monasticism. The friars built a wooden church and friary next to the south entrance of the city in 1234. Henry III gave them timber from Kenilworth to shingle their oratory. Later Edward, the Black Prince, gave stone from his quarry in Cheylesmore to build a second stone church, begun in 1359. The tower of this second church still survives.

Many notable Warwickshire families supported this church and

An 1860s engraving of Christchurch.

brotherhood, families such as the Hastings and the Montalts (also called Montauld and Mould) who were buried within the original central towered church. Coventry's first mayor John Ward was also buried here. Some lay in the robes of the friars, considered a sure way of getting into heaven. The Grey Friars was surrendered to the crown on 5 October 1538. The guardian and his ten brothers then left the house and were given no pensions as the King believed that, as they had spent their lives begging, they could continue to support themselves thus. The church and friary were acquired by the council who eventually demolished everything except the tower and spire of the church. This tower stood alone in an apple orchard for many years and at one time was used as a pig sty, thus becoming known as the tallest pig sty in England.

In 1830 it was decided to rebuild the body of the church and in June 1831 the *Coventry Herald* reported that the rebuilding was coming to an end and the old ball, cross and vane had been removed from the spire for regilding by local artist Mr Cherry: 'the lower part of the ball was much battered by shot, and the vane perforated in four places by bullets, whether done by Cromwell or some modern marksman is a matter of conjecture'. The fact that the ball and vane could be seen from the barracks may answer this question. The church was reopened as a chapel of ease for St Michael in 1832 and called Christchurch. This church's life came again to an end in 1941 when the main body of the rebuilt church was destroyed by fire bombs. In the early 1950s the ruins were demolished, leaving for the second time in its history just the tower and spire.

CITY WALL

The city wall began as a concept in January 1329 when Edward III gave the prior and the good men of Coventry the right to duty on goods for sale in the market for a period of six years. This duty or murage – wall tax – would be used to build a wall to totally enclose the city. John de Eltham afterwards extended the period by two years, to save his own purse. Work eventually began on the wall in 1356 when the city annals record: 'Ric. Stoke, Mayor. He laid the firs stone at Newgate, and there began the Town Wall, which was forty years a building.' Some sources say the wall was begun in 1355 which could also be within the mayoralty of Richard Stoke.

The wall continued very slowly from New Gate (London Road) generally in a clockwise direction and on 20 November 1363 Edward III confirmed his charter and the work really got under way. The following year Edward gave licence to tax all traders in the city and all the inhabitants, initially except Coventry Priory. Further taxes were raised and in 1385 the wall began to enclose Cheylesmore manor house at the request of King Richard II. The

A nineteenth-century engraving of Swanswell Gate.

stone for this and Greyfriars Gate and Spon Gate was from the royal quarry at Park Hollows, Cheylesmore. The wall began to be built on priory land in 1404 – the prior began to complain about loss of finance from the time it was built. In a letters patent of Henry V dated 11 May 1417 the wall appears to have been nearing completion. The letter states that the city fathers had no land rents to pay for its completion and to help had made collections from the poor. In 1423 it was ordered that all the city gates should be completed. In that same year it was ordered that Hill Street Gate be made new and new

Mill Lane Gate.

gates, roof tiles and doors added. In 1437 Bablake Gate was leased for ninety-nine years to the Trinity Guild who maintained nearby St John's church. The rent was one red rose to be payable to the mayor and chamberlains on the feast of John the Baptist. In 1441 Will Oxton, sergeant at mace, was to repair Bishop Gate. During the Wars of the Roses the gates were defended for we are told that, after Edgecote Field, a serpentine with a chamber (a chamber-loaded cannon) was delivered to New Gate, also a hand gun (a hand cannon) and a fowler. For Bishop Gate there was a staff gun and a fowler, a long barrelled gun with spread shot. In 1471 Cheylesmore Gate was armed with a cannon and hand cannon. In 1480 the Derne or Bastille Gate also known as Mill Lane Gate was mentioned.

Some modern sources would have us believe that the wall was unfinished from Swanswell Gate to Gosford Gate. This makes no sense as in the mid-fifteenth century on two occasions the royal army of over 30,000 men was encamped outside this section and was unable to enter the city when Edward called Warwick to battle. It has been said that the last section of the wall was the work of one mason and took 104 years to build. The wall was in fact rebuilt on a different alignment to suit the prior, who wanted it to take in the Pool Meadow area, site of St Osburg's Pool and the priory fish ponds. The original line of the wall here followed the course of the river running from a minor gate near the present Old Fire Station. Parts of this wall have been discovered in the past, especially in the 1930s during excavations by J B Shelton. When the prior complained about the murage in 1480 he was told by the mayor that if parts fell into disrepair it was down to him to sort them out, adding that the city had already been put to a great expense by moving the wall to please him! Excavations on a section near Gosford Gate thought to have been completed before 1410 gave a date in the 1520s and 1530s but this is likely to be a rebuilding due to the close proximity to the river making it unstable. Wall foundations would have been rebuilt and ditches scraped, leaving only the evidence of later work.

The completed wall measured nearly 2½ miles around and had twelve gates. It was between 8 and 9 feet thick and varied between 12 and 15 feet tall. The five main gates were Bishop Gate, Gosford Gate, New Gate, Greyfriars Gate and Spon Gate. The minor gates were Cook Street Gate, Swanswell Gate, Bastille Gate, Little Park Gate, Cheylesmore Gate, Bablake Gate and Well Street Gate. Between these many gates, built over a period of time, the wall was interspersed with thirty-two square and round towers, for defence. At most points within a few feet of the wall was a ditch up to 25 foot across which was regularly scraped and could be quicklyy filled with water using splayers connected to the Sherbourne and Radford Brook.

During the Commonwealth the manor and park of Cheylesmore became the property of the mayor and commonalty of Coventry. On the restoration of Charles II the corporation sought to find favour with the new monarch by handing the manor, its parks and various rents back to the King – along with a silver ewer and basin which cost 150 guineas to sweeten the King. The ploy however did not work and Charles, mindful of the fact that the walled city had repelled his father and held for Parliament, gave away the lease of the

Spon Street Gate.

manor and park to Sir Robert Townsend and ordered the city walls to be levelled. It was also suggested that the King ordered that a huge mound be raised in the park and planted with an elm to mark the place where his father stood on the day of his rejection.

Accordingly, on 22 July 1662, the earl of Northampton with a large number of local knights and gentry entered the city. They were welcomed by the mayor who had to bite his tongue as the earl of Northampton symbolically breached the wall at New Gate which had held against his royal majesty. Work thereafter began in earnest as a number of county troopers began to make breaches in the wall. Over the next three weeks and three days 500 men were employed in the process of destruction, at a cost of £500.

In 1662 Greyfriars Gate was made into a dwelling. At the end of October 1781 it was reported that during work to demolish Greyfriars Gate part of the stonework fell upon two workmen, dangerously wounding one in the head and the other in the back. In the Court Sessions of 1675 we find a reference to Cheylesmore Gate and wall being pulled down by Sir Robert Townsend. In June 1786 Swanswell Gate was up for sale. The auction, to take place at the Rose and Crown in the High Street, included, 'Two new freehold tenements, situate near to Swanswell, and formerly part of a building called Stour Gate; together with the wall, called the Town Wall, and a piece of ground . . . known by the name of the Town Ditch . . .'

When the site of Gosford Gate was excavated in the 1930s it was found to have been built on oak piles going down 14 feet. This instability was probably due to the nearby river and flooding (as noted above). In 1858 the archway of Swanswell Gate was filled in and the building was first occupied by a greengrocer.

☛ *See* **SIEGE OF COVENTRY**

COACHES

The first coach to run directly from Coventry to London ran from the Cross Keys in Earl Street on 7 August 1750 for 'reasonable terms'. Previously passengers had to catch the slower Chester to London coach as it passed through the city. Many of the main coaching routes, such as the London Road and the Holyhead Road, had their steepest hills cut down or winding routes shortened for the convenience of the coach. For example, the route of the London Road which once passed across Whitley Bridge was changed in 1832 to cut that section off. Also the steep hill at Toll Bar End by the old Toll Gate was lowered. One cottage survives there and is particularly noticeable because it stands higher than the later buildings as it once stood upon the hill top.

Coaches ran from the city's largest inns such as the White Bear, later the Craven Arms, and the King's Head. Coventry's best known independent coaching office was under the proprietorship of Amos Packwood in the High Street. In 1810 Packwood ran the London Union Post Coach from Coventry to London at 5.45 pm every Wednesday and Friday, arriving in London the following morning. The Bristol Telegraph Post Coach left High Street every morning at 11 am, except Sunday, and arrived in Bristol at 3 am the following day. The Leicester Telegraph Post Coach left for Leicester every evening at six and arrived there four hours later. Like the daily Birmingham

One of Dan Claridge's coaches outside the Craven Arms in the late 1870s.

coach, the Royal Charlotte Post Coach took three hours to Birmingham.

Packwood also transported parcels, packages and goods by running fly wagons such as the London, Bristol, Leicester and Birmingham fly wagons, huge canvas covered vehicles pulled by a team of six horses. By 1825 others had entered the market, the roads had improved and the trip to London was reduced by coaches such as the 'Wonder' which left Coventry at 11.15 am and arrived in London that same evening.

COINAGE

It is recorded that there was a mint in the city in the twelfth century under the control of the earl of Chester and the bishop of Coventry. That said, no coins from this period can as yet be attributed to this early mint. It was probably Christmas 1465 when King Edward IV gave Coventry the right to strike its own coins. The gold and silver coins were part of his new 'light' coinage and bore the letter 'C' under the king's head. On the reverse were the words 'CIVITAS COVENTRE' and the coinage consisted of gold ryals, half ryals, silver groats and half groats. The traditional site of this mint is where the Golden Cross public house stands on the corner of Hay Lane.

In the seventeenth century the shortage of small change caused many traders to issue small copper tokens, which usually bore the name of the issuer followed by 'his (or her) Halfpenny' and a symbol of their trade or sign of their inn. In 1669 the corporation issued its own halfpenny and farthing, banning all other private tokens. This new token bore the elephant and castle and the legend, 'A COVENTRY HALFE PENNY 1669'. Three years later all tokens were dropped when Charles II introduced new copper halfpennies and farthings. In 1792 another shortage of small change led to the reintroduction of halfpenny tokens. These, minted in Birmingham, were stamped on the side with words like, 'Payable at the warehouse of Robert Reynolds'. These tokens bore on one side Lady Godiva and on the obverse either the Coventry Cross or more commonly the elephant and castle copied off the seventeenth century mayor's chair in the Old Council Chamber in St Mary's Hall.

A Coventry minted groat from the reign of Edward IV.

COOPER, EDWARD WARD

History tells us that in 1868 Rowley Turner, the nephew of Josiah Turner, brought the first boneshaker cycle to Coventry, rode it from Coventry station to the Coventry Sewing Machine factory, causing quite a stir in the city. Thereafter the first cycles were produced in the city at the factory. However, in 1908 E W Cooper published his memoirs in the press and told another story.

Cooper was educated at the Blue Gift School and after leaving worked for a small engineering firm. While there he began to construct his own steam engine in his own time. He needed a fly wheel and went to the European Sewing Machine Company looking for one. Here he met and was helped by James Starley of cycle fame. Later Cooper went to Starley's factory in King Street looking for work. He was turned away but called back when Starley recognized him. Soon the firm was renamed the Coventry Machinist Company and moved to Cheylesmore.

Cooper and Starley got on well and soon Cooper began to work at Starley's side. Then the cycle arrived, not with Rowley as he was still in France, but crated up in a railway delivery van. Cooper recalls,

We all gathered around Mr [Josiah] Turner, our manager – Ole Starley the mechanical genius – myself and a few awe struck officials. We listened in profound silence while the manager explains that his nephew on the continent has 'sent to Coventry' the marvel of the age – a velocipede – that when mounted and propelled by the rider turning the cranks with his feet, will take him along at a speed often mile per hour.

Edward Cooper and his wife and dog at home in 1916.

Starley grabbed the cycle and carried it into the open yard and said to Cooper, 'Get on it. I'll hold the brute, I'm married and have a family.' Cooper recalled, 'I climbed into the saddle somehow and tried to wind the thing up with my feet, but as no impetus was given by even a push off, I simply tied myself and the blessed machine into a knot and came to earth without moving a couple of yards.'

Starley took the machine back and the following day it was brought out again onto a quiet inclined section of the Warwick Road. Cooper recalled, 'Again I mounted the steed, and with a prodigious shove off I kept my seat (without peddling) for quite a distance, and then, well I came off.' After several hours Cooper slightly improved, except for the fact that his shins were badly cut and bleeding. Within a week with the help of leather shin protectors Cooper had mastered the machine and even placed an extra seat on the machine for his sweetheart Elizabeth. He wrote, 'Very soon my inamorata learned to ride side saddle at my back, being the first lady, I believe to venture on a velocipede.' E W Cooper spent all his life in the cycle trade.

☞ *See* **BICYCLES (FIRST)**

CORPUS CHRISTI GUILD

This was the second most powerful guild in Coventry, formed in 1348. It met at St Nicholas Hall and its church was also dedicated to St Nicholas on Barrs Hill. Here priests prayed for the souls of departed guild brethren. The guild became fairly rich due to many wealthy supporters giving land and property to it.

In 1536 the Corpus Christi Guild were annexed to Holy Trinity Guild, probably for financial reasons as membership and rentals for Trinity Guild and Corpus Christi were dropping.

☞ *See* **ST MARY'S HALL**

COUNCIL HOUSE

Over previous centuries all council business was confined to St Mary's Hall. The present council house in Earl Street was designed by Birmingham architects Edward Garratt and H W Simister to blend in with St Mary's and St Michael's at the rear. During demolition and the following building work tons and tons of rubble and masonry were removed from the site of the old castle. The council house itself was erected between 1913 and 1917, taking longer expected because of the war. The intervention of the war also meant that the building wasn't officially opened by the duke of York (later George VI) until June 1920.

The building was faced with Runcorn stone and roofed with Cotswold stone. Over the entrance to the building is a rich array of figures including

Leofric, Godiva, Henry VI, the Black Prince and many other notables associated with the city. Inside the actual council chamber itself is a beautiful example of the arts and crafts movement with carved stalls representing the animals of the Forest of Arden. These were created under the supervision of Henry Wilson, president of the Arts and Crafts Exhibition Society. Wilson was also responsible for the smaller figures on the frontage of the building.

On the corner of the building with St Mary's Lane is a fine clock tower held within the wings of St Michael. Also on the tower can be seen Leofric and Justice, and Peeping Tom looking from a special niche in the corner. Despite the obliteration of the street opposite, the council house itself survived the blitz, apart from having every single front window broken. The façade of the building was also lacerated with holes and gashes caused by shrapnel, but it has gradually been restored over the years.

COUNTY OF COVENTRY

On 21 September 1451 Henry VI came to Coventry and conferred on it a great honour, making it a county in itself, the City and County of Coventry. The new county, separate from Warwickshire, was 30 square miles consisting of Coventry and the villages and hamlets of Radford, Keresley, Foleshill, Exhall, Ansty, Shilton, Caludon, Wyken, Henley, Wood End, Stoke, Biggin, Whitley, Pinley, Asthill, Harnell, Horwell, Whoberley and part of Walsgrave and Stivichall.

The county status meant that Coventry had to have its own assizes, its bailiffs were made sheriffs and the people of Coventry were made free from 'Toll, Passage, Murage and Pavage'. All was well until the government introduced the Municipal Reform Act of 1835 which saw the end of closed councils elected by freemen. In 1836 a new town council elected by ratepayers took control of the city. The Act also divided the city into six wards, the sixth ward being the villages and hamlets that made up the county of Coventry. This effectively meant that those villagers were expected to pay the same rates as their fellows in Coventry but without the advantages.

Many refused to pay and legal disputes flourished. In 1842 Parliament passed the Coventry Boundary Act which decreed that the City and County of Coventry should cease to exist and return back to the county of Warwickshire. Thus after nearly 400 years Henry VI's legacy to the city came to an end.

COVENTRY (THE NAME)

'Couaentree' is the earliest known spelling of Coventry and can be found upon a charter of Edward the Confessor. The first half of the word comes from 'Couaen' or 'Cune'. The Cune is the ancient name of the River

Sherbourne and the 'tree' or 'treabh' is said by place-name experts to mean a farmed village; so 'Couantree' should mean the farmed village by the River Cune.

'Cune' is also associated with places where waters meet, one such place being where the Og meets the Kennet which in Romano-British times was called 'Cunetio'. There is also Cound near Shrewsbury where the Cound meets the Severn. Coventry itself was once such a meeting place, with its central lake fed by the Sherbourne and the Radford Brook. Interestingly, these meeting places of waters also used to be sacred to the Celtic god 'Condatis'.

The name Cune appears regularly up until the sixteenth century. In the ancient Celtic tongue it can mean one of two things, 'Hound', or from 'Kuno', exalted holy river. The Saxon name for the River Sherbourne can also imply sacredness, translated as the 'sacred' or 'pure' river. This is not surprising, for all rivers whose localized source could be found coming from the ground were originally considered sacred. The 'Hound' cannot be totally dismissed either because there are other ancient hound names around the city such as 'Dog Land' and 'Hounds Hill'. These may suggest a lost name of a local tribal leader, the river being a sacred river marking the boundary of the 'Cunobelinus', Hound Lord's territory. The Saxon word for the Cune, the Schirebourne, can also mean boundary water. Coundon itself has an ancient site and in the past a high-grade Celtic bridle fitting from a horse which pulled a chariot was found here. It has also been previously suggested that the name Coundon actually means the 'fortress on the hill'.

In the past others have said that Coventry comes from the 'Convent Town', taking its name from St Osburga's monastic house. This would make it a rather late place-name and not likely. Another theory that has also rightly long since been dismissed is that the name comes from that a pact or 'Covenant' made here by two Danish warriors. A mid-Victorian tale if I've ever heard one!

The generally accepted modern version of the meaning of Coventry actually dates from the 1890s when an 'expert' decided it derived from 'Cofantreo' a word only ever found once in the Anglo Saxon Chronicle. The 'expert' decided if you drop the 'n' you are left with 'Cofa Treo' meaning Cofa's Tree or the tree of a person called Cofa. The problem with this is that Cofa is not a personal name and that 'Cofa' actually means heart. It is only used in conjunction with another word. So Cofa's Tree is another unlikely candidate.

Another contender for the name is 'Covan' or 'Coven' which is an Old English word referring to a cave, valley or cell. The settlement in the valley could be applied to Coventry, as the modern city has swallowed up a valley which once surrounded the great lake. The most likely explanation, however, lies with the Cune, the settlement at the meeting place of waters, although the Hound cannot be totally dismissed.

COVENTRY CANAL

In 1768 an Act of Parliament enabled the creation of a canal running from Coventry to Fradley Heath, where it would join another canal running from the River Trent. The main use of the canal at that time was to transport coal to feed the houses and manufactories which were now springing up in the towns. The first sod was cut in May 1768 and the great canal engineer James Brindley completed the canal quickly. On 10 August 1769 the city celebrated as the first two coal barges from Bedworth entered the new canal basin. The sum raised for the project amounted to £50,000 but this was only enough to fund the canal from Coventry to Atherstone. Further Acts of Parliament were needed to raise more money to continue the canal and link onto the Midland Network. By 1790 the network was completed. The canal was linked to four major rivers via the canal basin.

Coventry Canal Basin after restoration. Note the crane for unloading barges.

COVENTRY CAROL

In the Tailor's and Shearman's cycle of the Coventry Mystery Plays the audience witnessed the birth of Christ. In this sequence at the Nativity, as Mary cradled the Christ Child in her arms, the Coventry Carol was sung. The first verse of which goes thus:

> *Lully lulla, thou little tiny child,*
> *By by lully lullay*
> *O sisters too, how may we do,*
> *For to preserve this day*
> *This poor youngling, for whom we do sing.*
> *By by lully lullay.*

The song, probably written in the fifteenth century, then goes on to describe Herod's slaughter of the innocents. The Coventry Carol is still regularly performed today and is found in modern Christmas compilations.
☛ *See* **MYSTERY PLAYS**

COVENTRY CROSS

Deeds relating to Holy Trinity church property contain the first reference to a cross in the centre of Coventry. The document dating to 1300 refers to a property in the Spicer Stoke (a small lane leading from Broadgate towards Trinity) and mentions that the property stands 'ante crucem', before the cross. In a cartulary of St Mary's Priory from around 1400 the cross is mentioned again as the cross in the marketplace. Cross Cheaping itself takes its name from this, being the market (the cheaping) by the cross. The cross stood on the boundary between Broadgate and Cross Cheaping near the entrance to Spicer Stoke which is around the point where the present roadway cuts across the top of the flower bed in Trinity Street.

This first cross would have been, like others in the city, made of sandstone with a tall cross shaft supported by three or four steps. In 1423 it was decided that a new cross was needed in Cross Cheaping. This new cross stood on eight pillars and remained for over a hundred years before the upper section had to be removed when it became unsafe. The lower section stood for a number of years as the council discussed the idea of replacing it. Various city notables gave money towards the repair of the cross, but nothing was done, for many wanted it replaced instead. In 1541 Stoke-born Sir William Hollis, former mayor of London, left £200 for the building of a new cross. He also left instructions on the cross's design, saying it should be like the one in Abingdon (now in Oxfordshire), and was to be covered with figures of kings, saints and beasts.

A late nineteenth-century engraving by Webster showing how the Coventry Cross would have looked in the eighteenth century.

Cuthbert Joyner, the mayor, laid the first stone of the new cross in 1541 and when completed in 1544 it stood 57 feet high. Excelling all expectations it bore the figures of Henry VI, Edward I, Edward III, Richard I, Henry V, Henry III and King John, to mention a few. The cross after its completion was painted and gilded with gold leaf. Dugdale said of it: 'It is one of the chief things wherein this city most glories, which for its workmanship and beauty is inferior to non in England.'

In 1626 Thomas Sargenson, stone mason, and Thomas Bewdley, plumber, were asked to assess the cross's condition. They reported that it was now in some parts decayed. Work was done to repair the cross and it was newly painted and gilded. During the Commonwealth when the cross was threatened with demolition by puritan fanatics the butchers of Butcher Row stood against them. Colonel Purefoy ordered the cross's demolition but was talked out of it by Mayor Robert Beake, who got Purefoy to compromise by removing six sets of royal arms instead. In 1654 when John Evelyn visited he said of the cross: 'The Cross is remarkable for Gothic work and rich gilding, comparable to any I have ever seen.'

In 1688 the cross was again looking sad and a major restoration was set about, costing £323 4s 6d. During this restoration 15,403 books of gold were used to cover most of the cross. The result was that in bright sunshine the whole structure shimmered, frightening the horses, and it was also said that country people could hardly bear to look at it. The Coventry Cross became a nationally known landmark and a rhyme about it was written which is said to predate the Banbury Cross rhyme.

Ride a cock horse to Coventry Cross,
To see what Emma can buy,
A penny white cake,
I'll buy for her sake,
And a two penny tart or a pie.

In 1702 the cross again needed repair and it was assessed by noted sculptor Sir William Wilson. The work however was expensive and not carried out, probably because of financial problems associated with the Sir Thomas White Charity. In 1753 the upper part of the cross was in such a state it threatened to fall and had to be dismantled. Two years later it was lowered again to the height of the neighbouring houses. On 27 September 1771 it was recorded in the Common Council book: 'Agreed by the House that the Inhabitants of Cross Cheaping be at liberty; and they are hereby authorised if they see fit to take down the cross . . . '

Thereafter we are told that in 1771 Coventry Cross was demolished. This date was even recorded on tokens struck by antiquarian Thomas Sharp in the 1830s. Yet many other sources show that the cross was still standing some years later. In the *Coventry Mercury* on 27 January 1772 a case in mentioned in which a dragoon officer attacked a stranger with his sword at the Unicorn, an inn described as being 'near the Cross'. Also Alderman Hewitt in his journal records a confession in October 1772 when he writes that he 'desired it [a stout stick] to be brought up to the north side of the cross'. He also notes the confession of John Farn on 10 April 1773 that 'on that day this examinant bought below the cross, a pound of gunpowder'. Even later, in 1778, an anonymous writer states: 'The cross heretofore so famous for its workmanship, has no longer anything to please . . . and being much decayed, all the upper part was taken down about twenty years ago.' When traveller and naturalist Thomas Pennent came to Coventry in 1782 he makes no mention of the cross, so we can assume that it was demolished some time between 1778 and 1782.

COVENTRY CUPS

In the past it became normal for the mayor and city brethren to present a locally made gold or silver cup to a visiting monarch. The first recorded to receive this honour was hero of Agincourt, King Henry V, in 1420. Henry received £100 and a gold cup valued at £10 and a similar cup was presented to his queen. His son, the young Henry VI, received a similar gift in 1433, but this time the cup was silver gilt. In 1455 when Henry was older the city fathers gave him and his queen, Margaret of Anjou, a cup each weighing a total of 44 ounces.

Others to receive a cup were Edward, earl of March, Prince Edward, son of Edward IV, Henry VII and his eldest son Prince Arthur. In 1565 Queen Elizabeth I was presented with a purse containing 100 gold angels instead of the customary cup. The Queen was delighted, stating it was a 'Good gift, indeed'.

On Tuesday 3 April 1603, Princess Elizabeth, daughter of James I, was brought to the city by Sir John Harington of Coombe Abbey. The princess dined in St Mary's Hall and afterwards the mayor presented her with a double gilt silver cup, three-quarters of a yard high and costing £29 16s 3d. The princess, being so small, needed Sir John's assistance in receiving her heavy and tall gift.

A drawing of the Coventry Cup given to King James I.

On 2 September 1617 King James himself came to the city and, like his daughter, was entertained at St Mary's Hall. His was the most elaborate cup of all, weighing 45 ounces of pure gold and costing £172 – and if that were not enough, £100 in gold was placed within the bowl. This cup was of a particularly elaborate design and the King promised to drink from it wherever he went. He ordered it to be placed with the royal plate so it would be preserved forever.

In 1660 the council broke the tradition and sent a silver basin to Charles II, who was not impressed with such a gift from a city which had affronted his father. On 1 September 1687 James II came to the city. He, like James I, was presented with a fantastical cup which cost the corporation £171 17s 6d. King James on receiving the cup immediately gave it away to Lord Dartmouth, saying, 'I would have your Lordship receive this cup and cover as a mark of the City of Coventry's concern for your father.' Lord Dartmouth's father, Colonel Legge, had been captured at Worcester and imprisoned in Coventry Gaol until he made an escape. After this affront the city of Coventry never presented another cup.

COVENTRY EVENING TELEGRAPH

The *Coventry Evening Telegraph* was first published as the *Midland Daily Telegraph* on Monday 9 February 1891. The paper was founded by William Issac Iliffe (1843–1917), the son of a Coventry bookseller and printer. As Coventry was the heart of the cycling industry in 1879 he launched *The Cyclist* and soon after relaunched *Bicycling News*. This was followed by various journals including the well known *Autocar*, edited by Henry Sturmey, famed for the Sturmey–Archer gears.

In 1879 Illife took over the *Coventry Times* and in February 1891, with his partner Henry Sturmey, first released the evening paper the *Midland Daily Telegraph,* selling for a halfpenny a copy. This was joined by the Saturday evening sports *Pink* in July 1891.

In 1905 the Iliffe/Sturmey partnership ended and the *Telegraph* continued solely under the Iliffe family. William died in 1917 and the business passed to his sons, William Coker Iliffe and Edward Iliffe, who soon after was knighted. Shortly after the war the *Midland Daily Telegraph* became the *Coventry Evening Telegraph,* being edited and printed in Coventry in Corporation/Upper Well Street and at its best its daily sales were over 126,000 copies.

Over the last twenty years the paper has passed from one proprietor to another and in 2006 print production finally stopped in Coventry. The *Telegraph* is no longer an evening newspaper.

COVENTRY PRIORY

Coventry Priory or the Priory and Church of St Mary appears to have been built upon the site of St Osburga's nunnery on the hillside near Hill Top. The monastic houses were probably built there because there appears to have been a water source lying above them which could feed running water through the site for use in the various buildings. The water course was still in existence in the seventeenth century, for in the Coventry Constable Presentments on 8 April 1678 we find Thomas and William Shakespeare fined, 'for not paying their parts or shares towards repairing the watercourse in Trinity church yard'. Once this water had been used for drinking, washing, cooking and toilets it ran out of a drain into the Sherbourne below the site.

The generally accepted idea that Leofric and Godiva actually founded Coventry Priory is questionable, mainly because the charters that claim this are later forgeries created to win benefits for the monks. Interestingly, we are told that Godiva's father confessor talked her into founding a house of Benedictine monks in Coventry. There was of course already the established house of St Osburga's and it was to this house in 1022 that Canute gave the arm of St Augustine. John Leland, quoting ancient sources, wrote in the sixteenth century that the site of Coventry priory was formally the place where 'Kynge Canute the Dane made [a] house of nunes. Leofrike, Erle of the Marches, turnyd it in Kyng Edward the Confessors's dayes into a howes of monkes.' The church and abbey was Coventry's Benedictine monastery, which was dedicated by Edsi, archbishop of Canterbury, to God, the Virgin Mary, St Peter, St Osburg (the original dedication) and All Saints. The monastery housed an abbot and twenty-four monks and within its church (later cathedral) were housed the relics of St Augustine and St Osburga.

The cathedral seems to have been built mainly from the twelfth to fourteenth century and was 400 to 425 feet long and entered through a red and white doorway, down three semi-circular steps. Along the side of the building were a number of chapels and, at the east end, three chevet chapels, making it one of the largest in England. Going north down the hillside towards the river was a range of buildings including the great hall, the chapter house and many others, including water mill. For many years it has been thought that the cathedral looked almost identical to its sister church in Lichfield, having three spires. This theory, generally taken as fact, did not actually appear until 1718, when Willis Browne first suggested it his book on mitred abbeys. This idea seems to stem from the seal of Roger Longspere de Meulan from 1258, which in fact shows the bishop standing before two stylized churches, both of which may have three frontal spires (or pointed architecture), also a central spire topped with a large ball.

The only seal (now gone) which did actually show St Mary's church

Excavations of the priory undercroft off Hill Top, photographed in July 2001.

portrayed a building with two front towers and a central tower topped off with short cupolas and pinnacles. It was also noted during recent excavations of the site that the central tower could not have supported a spire, nor was there any evidence that one had been demolished. The idea of a three-spired church was dropped by those in the know by the mid-nineteenth century. Warwickshire historian William Reader realized the mistake after his *New Coventry Guide* was published. He wrote in his personal copy, in the section stating that the priory looked like Lichfield: 'Error – the seal of the Priory. It had towers – but no spires.'
☛ *See* **PILGRIMS**

COVENTRY TAPESTRY
In St Mary's Hall, Bayley Lane, can be seen the greatest surviving relic of the cult of King Henry VI left in England. The north window is called the King's Window and depicts Henry VI and his ancestors. Outside the hall niches once held statues mirroring these images. For eighty years after Henry's death he was venerated as a saint in England. Henry VII started off the canonization by sending a list of 300 miracles and 174 wonders to the Vatican.

King Henry VI taken from the Coventry Tapestry.

Representatives from Rome came to England to talk to the people involved in these claims and many miracles were verified.

Two Popes told Henry VII that they could complete the canonization if he gave them more money. Henry VII was not noted as a money giver and declined, asking them to continue at their own pace. They did and soon Henry died and was followed by Henry VIII. In 1526 the latter made an offering at the shrine of Henry VI in Windsor but by 1539 he had split with Rome and started the Dissolution, which saw the end of the chances of St Henry's final canonization.

Although the cult of Henry VI is now generally a forgotten piece of history, in its time it eclipsed both the cults of Edward the Confessor and Thomas à Becket. By the year 1500 the most venerated images in England were the Virgin Mary and King Henry VI, the 'Light of the World'.

The first shrine to Henry outside of London was at York Minster where a screen was created showing Henry and his ancestors. Before this screen people prayed. In Coventry the same was done at St Mary's Hall, with the statues and the King's Window. Add to this the 30 foot Coventry Tapestry, created around 1495 to 1500, probably according to Ingrid De Meuter, conservator of tapestries and textiles at the Museum Royal in Brussels, by the Flemish artist Roger Vander Weyden.

The tapestry not only commemorates St Henry but also his royal court as it was when it was based in the city for nearly three years during the Wars of the Roses. It contains many identifiable figures, such as the great Lancastrian knight John Talbot, who stands full bearded (as he does on his tomb) with his son John Lord Lisle, who was made lord treasurer in Coventry and here shows his purse. Both are identifiable by the white Talbot dog standing beside them, an image used in connection with the Talbots a number of times in late medieval art. The king's great uncle Henry Beaufort can be seen and Henry and Queen Margaret's favourite William de la Pole, duke of Suffolk.

The saints that cross the top of the tapestry at times link in with the figures below. In the case of Suffolk, the minor saint St Adrian has amazingly pushed St Peter into the background. This is totally against all the known rules of church art. St Adrian, patron saint of brewers, is a soldier and Suffolk was a soldier for forty years. He stands on a lion, a symbol of fortitude which is also the badge of the duke and he holds a block and sword, symbols of his execution and martyrdom. The block and sword were also linked to Suffolk as these were used in his illegal execution at the hands of Yorkist pirates. Other saints linking into the figures below are royal St Catherine, pointing at her fellow royal Henry. Thaddeus, patron saint of lost causes, points his bill at Prince Edward who was murdered after the battle of Tewkesbury and thus himself a lost cause. In the top centre can be seen the seated figure of Justice which has been placed over a previous image of Christ in Glory wearing a red robe and seated on a throne. This alteration may have been done in 1519 when it is recorded that, after discussion with the mayor and his brethren, some men 'mended' the tapestry. Mended may actually be 'amended', for during this year people were being burnt in Coventry because of their beliefs.

Queen Margaret of Anjou kneels opposite Henry, with an apple tree for Anjou before her and a French chateau. The apples are also a theme in the border, with red Lancastrian roses. She wears a headdress covered in tear drop and black pearls, symbols of mourning, for both Henry and her son Edward were murdered. Above her stands St Barbara with her White Tower, which is where Margaret spent her last days in England. Held above Henry is the sword, symbol of the murdered monarch, and in each corner of the tapestry is the monogram 'H&M' for Henry and Margaret. The Coventry Tapestry is the last major vestige of the veneration of Henry VI left in England and marks Coventry's greatest moment when it became home not only to the royal court but also to one of England's most noted saints.
☛ *See* HENRY VI

CROMWELL, OLIVER

None of the several versions of Coventry's city annals that exist mention Oliver Cromwell's visits to the city. One can only assume that he was later cut out by pro-Royalist writers. Where Cromwell stayed is unrecorded, possibilities include Whitefriars and Palace Yard, or even the Mayor's Parlour in Broadgate. What we can say for sure is that he attended St Michael's church and visited St Mary's Hall where the Committee of Safety was based. Cromwell did in fact visit Coventry a number of times and spent some time here. On 18 May 1645 Cromwell wrote from his unidentified lodging in Coventry regarding a union between himself, Fairfax, Brereton and the Scots, saying, 'then I know not why we might [not] be in as hopeful a posture as ever we were, having the King's army between us, with the blessing of God to bring him into great straights'. During this or his next visit Cromwell met Richard Baxter, a noted clergyman. Cromwell invited Baxter to be chaplain to his regiment which he accepted. After he visited the battlefield at Naseby Baxter wrote:

> *We that lived quietly in Coventry did keep to our old principles. We were unfeignly for King and Parliament. We believed that the war was only to save Parliament and Kingdom from papists and delinquents, and to remove dividers, that the King might again return Parliament; and that no changes might be made in religion. But when I came to the army among Cromwell's soldiers, I found a new face of things which intimidated their intention to subvert both the church and state. I was loath to leave my studies and friends and quietness of Coventry to go into an army so contrary to my judgement.*

During another visit Cromwell was approached by Dr Grew of St Michael's church who expressed his concerns for the King's safety. Cromwell assured him that the King would not die for his intention to the end was to put him back on the throne, but better controlled. When Charles was put on trial Grew wrote to Cromwell reminding him of their conversation. Cromwell did not reply.

In 1651 during the Second Civil War the uncrowned Charles II led a Scottish army into England. Coventry was put on alert and refortified. On 25 August Cromwell again entered the city, followed by an army under General Lambert and Harrison. As Charles approached the area he had intelligence of Cromwell's army at Coventry and veered off towards Worcester. Cromwell pursued and crushed the Royalist army there and sent hundreds of prisoners back to walled Coventry, finally ending the English Civil War. In 1657 bells rang and services were held in all Coventry churches to give thanks that a plot to kill Cromwell, Lord Protector, had been foiled.

☛ *See* **SEIGE OF COVENTRY**

CROW MOAT

Crow Moat was a large moated house, set within 100 acres, which once stood at the end of Crow Lane, off Spon Street. The first building on the site may date back to the twelfth or thirteenth centuries, belonging to part of the early suburb of Spon. It was possibly the property of Richard de Aula in the thirteenth century. Its first known owner was Adam Hyton, a wealthy dyer and mayor of the city in 1418. Hyton had acquired most of his properties and land off one John Burgeys. The building is described as the 'Crow Moat Hall' in deeds from 1468. After Hyton's death the building was acquired by his son's widow Joan, who remarried into the Bentley family who then owned the estate and its moated house. Afterwards the estate was split between the Bentleys and the Shirewoods and later came into the hands of Edmund Ratcliff.

In the early sixteenth century the moated house and its estate were claimed by none other than the grand prior of the knights hospitallers, one Thomas Docwar, who claimed a connection through the second son of Adam Hyton. A legal battle went on for some time in various courts and it is said that even Crow Moat Hall itself was attacked by armed hospitaller knights who tried to take it by force for the prior.

The outcome of the various battles was that the estate was split between the two parties. In the mid-sixteenth century the land and moat, apparently minus the house, belonged to the Temple family until they were sold by the family in 1627.

CYCLES

In the summer of 1861 James Starley arrived in Coventry and with Josiah Turner and others set up the Coventry Sewing Machine Company in King Street. Sussex-born Starley was an inventive genius and quickly began work on improving the sewing machine. In 1866 Josiah Turner's nephew Rowley Turner sent a Michaux cycle or boneshaker from France to the King Street factory and within a year the company was producing its own cycle called the 'Coventry Model'. Around the same time the company changed its name to the Coventry Machinist Company and opened a new factory in Cheylesmore. The CMC would later produce the popular 'Swift' cycle and then rename themselves the Swift Cycle Company. Starley and William Hillman split the company in 1870 and began making their own designs, the first of which was Starley's 'Aerial', the first all metal framed, geared penny farthing. This cycle was so common it acquired the name of the 'Ordinary'.

Next Starley produced the 'Wonder' and, after falling off it on Knightlow Hill, invented the differential gear which is found on all modern vehicles. In June 1881 he was summoned by Queen Victoria to personally deliver to her two Salvo Quad tricycles, afterwards this tricycle was renamed the 'Royal Salvo'. Later that summer Starley died at his home in Upper Well Street. He was considered the father of Coventry's cycle industry and it was thanks to him that Coventry went from the depression caused by the collapse of the weaving and watch trade and became the greatest cycle manufacturer in the world.

In 1876, when the 'Ordinary' was at the height of its popularity, Harry Lawson designed a chain-driven 'safety' cycle. Gradually all cycle manufactures based their 'safety' cycles on Lawson's design, eventually making both wheels the same size. In 1885 John Kemp Starley, nephew of

An 1887 advertisement for the Coventry Machinist Company.

COVENTRY MACHINISTS' Co.'s
"CLUB" CYCLES.

The SPORTSMAN, 29/1/87, says:—"The finish of these beautiful specimens is so good that praise is superfluous."

Works—COVENTRY.

The "SWIFT" SAFETY.
The leading Safety Bicycle. With Patent Non-vibrating Spring Forks.

LONDON .. .. 15 and 16, Holborn Viaduct.
MANCHESTER .. 9, Victoria-buildings.

The "MARLBORO'" No. 1.
With Patent Non-vibrating Spring Forks.

Agencies in all Principal Towns.   Catalogues, two stamps.

James Starley, produced his 'Rover' safety cycle, with a diamond shaped frame and pneumatic tyres, the first true modern cycle. By the 1890s over 40,000 people worked in Coventry's cycle industry and up until the 1930s there had been 248 cycle companies based in the city. Of these companies the firm Hillman, Herbert & Cooper advertised themselves as the world's largest manufactures, producing 40,000 cycles in 1897 alone. By 1954 the Coventry Eagle Company was the only Coventry manufacturer to survive.

☛ *See* **BICYCLE (FIRST), EDWARD WARD COOPER, RUDGE**

D

DICKENS, CHARLES

Charles Dickens visited Coventry on two occasions. The first was on Tuesday, 15 December 1857. On this brief visit he gave a reading, prompted by Sir Joseph Paxton, to a large assembly to raise funds for an artisans' institute in Hertford Street. Considering the time of year, Dickens chose to read his *Christmas Carol*. It was written afterwards:

> *Who could be better fitted for such a task than the author himself? Mr Dickens was clear and well sustained with dramatic power of expression, which gave a rapid and distinct individuality to the personages of his fancy in succession from Old Scrooge to Tiny Tim, and moreover, as might have been expected, every touch of humour and pathos,*

Charles Dickens.

> *which belongs to Dickens' own peculiar style, received from his delivery the whole meaning and point.*

On this visit it was said that the coach Dickens travelled on rumbled past Whitefriars Gate in Much Park Street. Dickens himself is said to have told a friend that he used it in *The Old Curiosity Shop* in a night-time scene when Little Nell stood in the shadows of the gate while Quilp dismounted a coach as the bells of St Michael's chimed. He also described Coventry itself:

> *a pretty large town, with an open square, and in the middle of which was a Town Hall [market hall] with a clock tower [market tower clock] and weather cock. There were houses of stone, houses of red brick, houses of yellow brick, houses of lath and plaster, houses of wood, very old and withered, faces carved upon the*

beam [the timbered house next to St Mary's has such a face carved on one of its beams] and staring down into the street. Many of the houses overhung the pavement. A few idle men lounged about the two inns, and the empty market place, and the tradesmen's doors, and some people were dozing in chairs outside the almshouse wall.

Dickens's second visit was by special invitation to be honoured by a dinner at the Castle Hotel in Broadgate on 5 December 1858. After many toasts were made to him he was presented with a gold Coventry-made watch inscribed with these words: 'Presented to Charles Dickens by his friends in Coventry, as a grateful acknowledgement to his kindness to them, and of his eminent services in the interest of humanity. December 1858.' Afterwards the large group of notables strolled with Mr Dickens to St Mary's Hall, taking a tour of the building in which Dickens showed much interest. Dickens is said to have kept his Coventry watch all his life.

DUGDALE, SIR WILLIAM

Although not actually born in Coventry, the great Warwickshire antiquarian was educated at the Free Grammar School on the corner of Bishop Street. During the Civil War Dugdale acted as the king's herald and was the man who requested Charles's entrance into the city, which was partly refused, leading to the siege. Also, because of his great knowledge of the highways and byways of Warwickshire, Dugdale was used by the royal army as a guide while it was in the county. His most notable achievements are however his books: the *Monasticon*, a history of monasticism, and his *Antiquities of Warwickshire*, which was illustrated by Wencelas Hollar and published in 1656. This is the first major history of the county of Warwickshire, the forerunner of all modern-day county history books.

☛ *See* **SIEGE OF COVENTRY**

E

ELECTIONS

Coventry elections at times have been extremely violent and needed an Act of Parliament to bring them under control. In the past only freemen, men who had served seven-year apprenticeships in the city, could vote. Tactics to control such votes could be excessive, as in the election of 1705 when a government injunction was acquired to preserve the peace in the election between Whig candidates, Orlando Bridgeman and Edward Hopkins, and Tory candidates, Sir Christopher Hales and Thomas Gery. With this injunction it was stated that no sticks should be carried during the election.

A political cartoon for a late eighteenth-century Coventry election.

Hopkins and Bridgeman agreed to this but Gery thought otherwise, telling the mayor, a Whig, that if he brought in constables he would bring in his own men carrying sticks to hold the peace.

On the evening before the election the mayor and aldermen summoned the constables and doubled the watch. At 2 am Gery began to raise his men and with a mob of up to 500 attacked the magistrates, constables and watch. The mayor was wounded and the constables and watch disarmed and dispersed. By 6 o'clock in the morning Sir Christopher Hales appeared and was said to have joined the mob and marched about the city in a 'riotous manner'. By 9 o'clock he had taken control of St Mary's Hall, where the votes were made, and held it for three days. Those who wished to vote for the Tory candidates were allowed in but those who wanted to vote Whig were lucky to escape the entrance to the hall intact. Many were unhorsed and beaten and one named Lightburn was dragged away, believed dead, beaten to oblivion with clubs. Those injured outside the hall included Sir Orlando Bridgeman himself and Mr Wade who represented Edward Hopkins.

Meanwhile the city sheriffs left control in the hands of the Tories. They did at the count suggest 'inspectors' should be present. To this Gery pointed to the mob saying, 'There are our inspectors'. The sheriffs backed down and, not surprisingly, Gery and Hales took the 1705 Coventry election. Afterwards the fur flew and the Tories indicted the Whigs for riot and vice versa. The case went to court and the election was quashed and refought in 1707, this time going fairly to Orlando and Hopkins.

This wasn't the end of election violence. In 1780 Lord Craven of Coombe Abbey, who supported Yeo and Holroyd, armed about 200 men with clubs to drive away the supporters of Halifax and Rogers from the polling booth. On 4 December 1780 a letter appeared in the *Coventry Mercury* stating:

> *Whereas a great number of Ruffians and Clodhoppers, who were hired by a certain noble Lord with a design by force and violence to beat and drive away the Freemen who were peaceably assembled around the booth on Wednesday morning last . . . when the said Ruffians and Clodhoppers will return to C-mb A-b-y, they will receive a free pardon for their cowardice . . .*

The extra constables who were brought in to control the election were outsiders and did nothing to stop the violence. It was afterwards discovered that 100 of them were servants and dependants of Lord Craven and they were led by Lord Craven's under-keeper. During this particular conflict the Tories were chased into St Mary's Hall and the Whigs gathered in White Horse Yard (now Castle Yard) next to the hall and threw brick and rocks through the fifteenth-century stained-glass windows.

Although by the mid-nineteenth century the violence had stopped, corruption according to some was still rife up to the First World War.

ELIOT, GEORGE

George Eliot was Mary Ann Evans, born at Arbury Farm near Nuneaton in 1819. Her early education took place in the Nuneaton area and from 1832 to 1836 her education was completed at the private school of Mary and Rebecca Franklin, daughters of the Revd Francis Franklin at 29 Warwick Row, Coventry. The Franklin sisters had a huge effect on the young Mary Ann, who based her speech and mannerisms on these educated ladies with Parisian ways. In her early years, although she had found an interest in writing, her mind was overtaken by a religious zeal which made her spend her time doing charitable works. At this point in her life Mary Ann Evans was probably destined to become a minister's wife. This all changed when, in 1841, her father retired to Bird Grove in rural Foleshill, taking 22-year-old Mary Ann with him. The Evans's neighbours, the Pears, introduced them to the Brays of Rosehill and Mary Ann's world changed forever. Mary Ann became extremely close to Charles and Cara Bray and Cara's sister Sarah Hennell. This helped her to look at the world with a more open mind and they also encouraged her, like them, to write. At the Brays' home Mary Ann also began to meet politicians, free-thinkers, philosophers and writers such as William Makepeace Thackeray.

The Brays questioned everything, including religion, and before long Mary Ann's began to question her own religious zeal, which resulted in her refusing to attend church with her father. Robert Evans threatened to have her sent away unless she did as she was told, but Mary Ann refused so she was sent back to Griff, the house she grew up in, by then occupied by her brother Isaac. After a number of conversations with the Brays, Franklins and Issac her brother, and knowing Mary Ann's mind, Robert Evans eventually relented and allowed Mary Ann back on condition that she attended church with him as a public show.

Mary Ann's first sojourn into the world of writing was the translation of *Leben Jesus* which was published in 1846. Other articles then began to be published in the *Coventry Herald* which Bray had acquired as a political mouthpiece. In May 1849 Mary Ann wrote to the Brays:

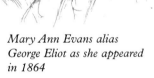

Mary Ann Evans alias George Eliot as she appeared in 1864

> *Dear Friends – Mr Bury told us last night that he thought father would not last till morning. I sat by him with my hand in his till four o'clock, and he then became quieter and has had some comfortable sleep. He is obviously weaker this morning . . . What shall I be without my father? It seems as if part of my moral nature were gone . . . P.S. – Father is very, very much weaker this evening.*

Robert Evans died that night in his Foleshill home.

After her father's death the Brays took Mary Ann on a long trip to the continent and she stayed on for some time in Geneva. When she returned she moved into Rosehill. Soon after she was invited to write for the *Westminster Review* and moved to London. Her closeness to the Brays was still evident for in 1852 Mary Ann wrote:

> *It is impossible that I should ever love two women better than I love you and Cara. Indeed it seems to me that I can never love any so well; and it is certain that I can never have any friend – not even a husband – who would supply the loss of the association with the past which belong to you.*

In 1857 her first novel *Scenes of Clerical Life* was published and two years later *Adam Bede*. Mary Ann, now under the alias George Eliot, kept quiet as to her authorship while a certain Mr Liggins bathed in its glory. On 20 June 1859, Mary Ann wrote:

> *We went to the Crystal Palace to hear the 'Messiah' and dined afterwards with the Bray's and Sarah Hennell. I told them I was the author of 'Adam Bede' and 'Clerical Scenes' and they seemed overwhelmed with surprise. This experience has enlightened me a good deal as to the ignorance in which we all live of each other.*

F

FARNDON, TOM

A generally forgotten local hero was Coventry-born Tommy Farndon, one of England's greatest speedway riders. In 1929 at the age of 18, while working for Rover, he applied for a trial at the newly opened Brandon Stadium. He was immediately taken on and made such an impact that in a year he was a member of the Coventry team, racing in the Southern League. He began to achieve even greater success when he moved to London and rode for Crystal Palace and New Cross. Tommy won the London Riders' Championship several times and the British Match Race Title and National Riders' Championship, then equivalent to the World Championship.

At one time in 1935 Tommy Farndon held the track record at every circuit in the national league. Applauded across the country and treated like a film star in Coventry, Tommy was on a high when he rode in the New Cross Stadium on 28 August 1935. In the final race team-mate Ron Johnson was leading, with Tommy close behind. Suddenly Johnson collided with the safety fence. Farndon swerved to avoid hitting his fallen team mate, but instead struck the bike. The resulting crash catapulted him over the bars and Tommy suffered from multiple head wounds. Two days later he died aged just 24.

On the day of his funeral New Cross Station was surrounded by thousands of fans. Tommy Farndon's body was brought back to Coventry where thousands more watched him on his last ride. This Coventry sporting giant was buried at St Paul's Cemetery in Holbrook's and his grave still stands out today, marked by a large black granite motorbike rider at speed.

FIRE SERVICE

Possibly the earliest mention of fire precautions in the city are in 1474 when the Leet Book names the men responsible for the fire hooks, rings, ropes and ladders. Coventry of course at this time had a number of thatched houses,

Fire crews posing outside Coventry's new fire station in 1903.

but most were tiled and no great conflagrations occurred in the city. In 1493 the Leet Book mentions another fire risk, forbidding chimneys made from tree trunks – these would often burst into flames and start fires. Later fire insurance companies were formed, such as the Sun and Phoenix. Houses of those who paid the fee bore a lead badge and in case of fire were protected by a small fire crew employed in the city. Originally their fire wagon was pulled by hand and later by horses. The only other fire teams in the city were found at the workhouse and at the barracks manned by the soldiers.

The city did not have its own fire service until its formation was prompted by a factory fire in Gosford Street in 1861. In fact that year a number of suspicious factory fires took place, leading to the formation of the Coventry Volunteer Fire Brigade, with the knock-on effect that the insurance fire companies became obsolete. They presented their manual engines to the Coventry service. This brigade was one of the first in the country and set up in St Mary's Street, next to the police station.

In 1872 a new steam pumping appliance was purchased and called the 'Sherbourne'. This was followed by more steam-powered horse-drawn engines, the 'Godiva' and 'Peeping Tom'. The latter, which was acquired in the 1890s, was still in working order in the 1940s. The force was totally voluntary and remained so until 1898 when a paid driver was employed, this man also doubled as a driver for the mayor when needed. Most of the staff however remained volunteers and in 1902 moved into the new main fire station with its own stables in Hales Street. At the end of the 1890s there were numerous major fires in the early car factories – whether this was due to lack of safety measures cannot be proved, but these fires were suspiciously regular and major. During this period many manufacturers formed their own works brigades. The City of Coventry Volunteer Fire Brigade became fifty years old in 1911 and in 1914 motorized pumps began to supersede steam as petrol engines replaced horsepower.

In 1916 many of the works brigades joined with the Coventry brigade to offer a better service and it wasn't until 1934, when the Hales Street Station was enlarged, that the service became professional. This new service, called the National Fire Service in 1941, did great service during the many bombing raids on the city. Many firemen lost their lives saving many others. In 1948 the Coventry Fire Brigade regained its regional independence and in 1974 it was replaced by the West Midlands Fire Authority who built a new headquarters at the bottom of the Radford Road.

FLYING WING

The Flying Wing was a highly advanced piece of engineering designed by the Armstrong Whitworth Aircraft Company. The wing was first conceived during the war and in 1946 an engineless glider version was towed by a Lancaster bomber, released and flew 15,000 feet above the company's factory at Baginton. The second version of the 100 foot wide wing flown in November 1947 was powered by two Rolls Royce Nene Engines, which were remarkably quiet as they were set deep within the wing. The wing was covered with a lightweight metal skin called 'Alcad' which was later brought back into use on the Concord and Vulcan. This plane travelled over 350 mph and during one test a shudder set in and the test pilot Jo Lancaster had to eject, making him the first man in history to use an ejector seat. The problems which caused the shudder were resolved with the next machine and the flying wing looked set to be the future, had the government not stopped funding the project, thus bringing it to a halt. The flying wing concept is now considered by many the future of flying.

FOOTBALL

Coventry City Football Club began life in 1883 as the Singer Football Club attached to the Singer Cycle works. It quickly became the most successful team in the city and in 1892 it was proposed that the team represent Coventry. On 12 August 1898, with permission from the Football Association, the Singer Football team was officially renamed Coventry City Football Club. The club first played at the Highfield Road site in 1899, when it was a field owned by the Craven Cricket Club and standing on the land of Highfield Farm. They registered the ground as Highfield Road with the

Coventry City FA: cup-winning players passing through the streets of Coventry on 19 May 1987.

league, despite the fact that it didn't actually stand in Highfield Road. The club's main offices were based near to the original entrance to the site. Coventry City won the FA Cup in 1987, against the favourites, Tottenham Hotspur. The Highfield Road ground was closed in 2005 and Coventry City Football Club transferred to its new Ricoh Stadium in Rowley's Green.

FORD'S HOSPITAL

Ford's Hospital in Greyfriars Lane was founded by merchant William Ford. The executor of his 1509 will, William Pisford Senior (probably Ford's father), considerably enlarged the original endowment. Pisford erected the present handsome building with its beautiful courtyard, using a large quantity of teak, a wood normally used on coastal buildings. With the money left by his son he purchased land to maintain the house for five 'aged men' and one old woman to look after them. These inmates were chosen by members of the Trinity Guild who maintained St Mary's Hall.

When William Pisford Senior died he willed that the alms house should

Ford's Hospital in Greyfriars Lane around 1911.

house six aged men and their wives, being aged 60 and above and of good name; also residents of Coventry who were in poverty. Each couple would receive seven and a half pennies a week for their needs. Should the wife die the man would receive the full sum for himself. Should the man die the wife would receive half the amount. Anyone who frequented alehouses or caused problems would, after three or four warnings, be put out by order of the Trinity Guild.

William Pisford also willed that a priest live on the premises and say mass for the founders and inmates. By the eighteenth century the hospital had become exclusively female and by 1817 it held seventeen aged women, each with their own room and a weekly payment of 4 shillings. A further twenty women also received a pension set up by the trust of William Pisford and his son. The hospital is still used today for its original purpose and was extended in the 1970s. Sadly, after 500 years, access to the courtyard is now restricted.

FORSTER, E M

College professor and novelist Edward Morgan Forster is famous for his novels such as *A Room with a View*, *A Passage to India* and *Howard's End*. Although Forster lived at King's College, Cambridge, the place he considered his real home was 11 Salisbury Avenue in Stivichall. Here lived his closest friends, his 'family' Bob and May Buckingham, who would regularly welcome Forster. While here Forster would take regular walks around the Memorial Park and was often visited by other notables such as Seamus Heaney, Benjamin Britten and Yehudi Menuhin. E M Forster died while in Coventry in 1970 and was laid to rest at Canley Crematorium.

FREEMEN

The term freeman of the city of Coventry derives from members of Coventry merchant guild who as such were free to trade in the city. Later, after the suppression of the guilds, freemen were men who had served an apprenticeship in the city and were given the right to vote and the right to restricted pasturage in the city. From the Municipal Corporation Act of 1835 a freeman had to serve a seven-year apprenticeship before applying to the mayor to be sworn in at St Mary's Hall as a freeman. Freemen of a certain age could claim 'Seniority Payment', a small pension raised from land held by the freeman's guild. This land which once surrounded the city had a direct effect on the city's growth, holding it back for many years, until the grip was broken and the land sold. By the late nineteenth century much of the freemen's land had been sold and the rights to pasture cattle on common land dropped. The freemen still meet in a small room under St Mary's Hall.

G

GAOL

The earliest reference to a prison or gaol in Coventry is in the 1230s when William Grom and others were taken and placed in Roger de Montalt's prison. All the prisoners escaped except for Grom who went into St Michael's church and pleaded sanctuary. The prison itself was most likely next door to St Michael, in what remained of Coventry Castle, which Montalt had inherited. It was not unusual for redundant castles to be used as prisons. The fact that prisoners escaped may reflect the poor condition of the castle remains in this period. It is known that the prior of Coventry also had a prison located on the northern side of the monastery.

In the charter of incorporation of 1345 Coventry was given the right to build a new prison situated in the earl's half of the city. Where exactly this was we do not know, but it may have been in Bayley Lane. In the sixteenth century a prison certainly stood in the top half of Bayley Lane next to the Gaol Hall. Because of the siting of the gaol the upper end of Bayley Lane became known as Gaol Lane (later Pepper Lane). It appears that the Undercroft of St Mary's Hall may also have been used as a prison in this period for the martyr Robert Glover said at the time: 'The second day after the bishop coming to Coventry, Master Warren came to the Guildhall, and commanded the chief gaoler to carry me to the bishop.'

The gaol was in a bad way and in 1698 was partly demolished. In the late eighteenth century Coventry mayor and magistrate John Hewitt ordered the prison's rebuilding, which was completed in 1776. In 1800 it was said of this prison, 'they had to sleep in noisome dungeons twelve steps below the ground, lighted by a window 11in. by 7in., and so foul that every other day torches with kettles of pitch and tar were burnt; while sleeping places of the debtors were fumigated with vinegar'.

In February 1829 the gaol held only thirteen people, who all tried to escape. The men made a hole through a cell wall and having removed iron bars from a chimney used them to hack their way through another wall, adjoining the street. Luckily as they were doing this a passer-by raised the alarm and the men were stopped and put in irons. In that same year it was decided to enlarge the gaol, a job which was completed in 1831. The new prison took in a large area between Pepper, Derby, Cuckoo Lanes and a small walkway along the side of Holy Trinity church. It consisted of 86 cells, eight day rooms and nine exercise yards. The gaol also had a treadmill which was adapted to grind barley and beans: worked by five prisoners it could grind six bushels a day. Those on the treadmill spent twenty minutes on and ten off and its use was believed to have 'beneficial effects'. In 1850 the turnkey and a women worker were involved in an attempted escape. A disguise was brought to the gaol but the escape was foiled. It was afterwards discovered that the turnkey was to be paid £120 for his work. Instead Coventry's turnkey got something else: fourteen years transportation.

The last inspection of the gaol took place in 1858 when it housed forty-three men and eight women. When Coventry lost its county status the prisoners were eventually all moved to Warwick Gaol and, after standing empty for some time, Coventry Gaol was finally demolished in May 1872. On its demolition a stone tablet was removed from one of the walls, it read:

MARY BALL/Aged 31/Executed for Murder/9th August, 1849
Mary Ball from Nuneaton was capitally convicted for the murder of her husband by poison. While in Coventry Gaol the prison chaplain held her hand

> **By authority of the Under-Sheriff.**
>
> THE
>
> # CONFESSION
> OF
> ## MARY BALL,
>
> As made to Mr. Stanley, Governor of the Gaol ; to which is added, an account of her Execution.
>
> On Thursday morning, August 9th, at an early hour, large crowds of people were observed flocking into Coventry from all directions to witness the execution, which took place at 10 o'clock precisely, in front of the Gaol.
>
> This wretched woman was tried and sentenced to be hanged at the last Coventry Assizes, July 28th, for the wilful murder of her husband, at Nuneaton, by administering to him a quantity of arsenic in a basin of gruel. During the trial, and for some days afterwards, she appeared to be indifferent to the awful situation in which she was placed. The Rev. H. Bellairs, Rector of Bedworth, visited her on the Tuesday after the trial, and used every effort to bring her to a sense of her awful position. He again visited her on Friday, and soon after his departure a change for the better was observable in the state of her feelings and conduct. On the same day she observed to Rebecca Vernon, a woman in waiting, that she had something to say, but that she would say it to the Governor, and no one else.
>
> On Sunday morning, she said to Rebecca Vernon that she liked to hear the Governor read, and that she wished to see him, he immediately waited upon her, and after reading to her a short time, she appeared anxious to say something, and taking him by the hand, she made the following confession :—

A handbill from 1849 referring to Mary Ball's execution outside Coventry Gaol.

over a candle to demonstrate to her what hell was going to be like. He was afterwards dismissed. Mary Ball was the last person hung in Coventry, on a temporary gallows set against the gaol wall. Her death was watched by thousands.

☛ *See* **JOHN HEWITT, COUNTY OF COVENTRY**

GEE, DAVID

David Gee was a local artist of some repute, who produced a small number of fine oil paintings of Coventry buildings and landscapes. Like many minor artists of his time he made most of his living from jobbing work, portraits, church painting and restoration and pub signs. His commissions for pub signs included the White Horse, Toby's Head, Craven Arms, George IV, Samson and Lion, Black Prince, Bablake Boy, Leopard and the Craven Arms in Binley. Sadly none of these signs survive, unlike some of his finer Coventry scenes which survive in the museum.

GILL, PADDY

William Gill was Coventry's most famed and successful prize fighter. He originated from Ireland, born in Dublin in 1819, hence the nickname 'Paddy'. He came to Coventry at the age of 5. As a young man he worked as a weaver and was in the habit of frequenting the Sword and Mace in Earl Street. Here he took an interest in prize fighting and caught the eye of the inn landlord, local sporting legend William King. King encouraged him into the sport and trained him in the art of fistiana. King also set up Gill's first fights. In the late nineteenth century, just before his death, King recalled that Gill 'bruised over some local nobodies and was then pitted against a big fellow called Foster, who he disposed of in a rattling fight, then knocked the buckram out of Hubbard'. Gill's second fight with Hubbard took place in deep snow. King said of it: 'it wor' almost deep enough to reach the knees of their fighting breeches. That wor' a day an' no mistake.'

Paddy's first fight took place in 1838 upon Radford Common for £5 a side against local fighter Bill Heap. The latter fought well but Gill proved the victor after fifty-five hard rounds. The more he fought the bigger his reputation grew, as did the purse. He fought Hubbard of Nuneaton in November 1842 for £25 a side. This battle proved a draw but Gill won the rematch, finishing Hubbard in forty-two rounds. He then moved on to the big time, fighting Norley of Manchester for £50 a side in October 1843. This bruising fight lasted one hour and fifty-five minutes, but Gill was outmatched and lost.

Despite this setback Gill won his next three fights, quickly finding himself back in the big league, matched against the London fighter, Reed the Invincible. Invincible he wasn't and Gill proved the victor, taking home a purse of £200. He then took on Norley again, this time for a massive purse of £500. The contest was fought at Whitney in Oxfordshire and lasted an extraordinary four hours and fifteen minutes. The fight had 160 rounds, meaning that at some point either man was beaten to the ground 160 times. The victor was Paddy Gill, who used part of his winnings to buy the Lamp Tavern in Market Street, Coventry.

In 1848 he fought the notorious Tom Maley in London and again walked away with the purse. Paddy was now seen as a national champion of fistiana. His strength and stamina were amazing but something went disastrously wrong: on 23 July 1850 Paddy fought Thomas Griffiths at Frimley Green and killed him. The following April he was put on trial for manslaughter and found not guilty, as all the witnesses protected Paddy and claimed they could not identify him. Paddy never quite recovered from this tragic event and soon gave up the ring, concentrating on being landlord of the Lamp Tavern. Life did not end particularly well for Paddy for he began to suffer mental problems, no doubt brought on by the beatings he had taken to the head. He was eventually placed into Hatton Asylum, near Warwick. Coventry's, and one of England's greatest prize fighters, William 'Paddy' Gill died in Hatton at the age of 50 in 1869.

GODIVA

Lady Godiva is one of the most recognized individuals in the world, not for what she did in her life but for what she might have done. Godiva, whose real name was Godgifu, meaning God's Gift, was the sister of Thorold, sheriff of Lincolnshire, born around the year 1000. The charter bearing this connection appears to have been written in the fourteenth century. This does not necessarily mean it is a fabrication as it may have been copied from an original document. The charter refers to Aelfgar as Godiva's eldest son, implying he had a brother. In the past that brother was said to have been the noted Hereward the Wake. As there are definite connections between Hereward and Leofric's family the idea cannot be totally dismissed as it has been in the past. There has also been speculation as to whether Godiva was really related to Thorold. This seems to be backed by the *Chronicon Petroburgense* which states under the date of 1050 that Thorold is a vice count and brother of Godiva.

It is believed that Leofric was Godiva's second husband and that the first may have been Earl Eglaf, who died around 1022 in Constantinople. Apart from the odd mention of bestowals and gifts Godiva is not mentioned in any chronicles of her own time. Most references to her appear from the fourteenth century. Ignulphus then, almost 200 years after her death, refers to her as being the most beauteous of all women of her time. Godiva is also mentioned with Leofric as giving gifts to many churches during Leofric's lifetime. After Leofric's death things got tighter, for Godiva visited Worcester personally to ask if she could keep until her death the lands Leofric had taken and promised to return on his demise.

Godiva would have been about 57 years old when Leofric died and Mercia reverted to their son Aelfgar. Godiva appears like many noble women of the time to have gone into retirement. On her death which, according to the 'Douce Manuscript', was in September 1067 she was laid at Evesham Abbey and not Coventry, as many much later writers claim. Up until 1038 Godiva had been a regular visitor to the abbey and church of Evesham which she and Leofric founded. The Evesham chroniclers claim that Godiva's father confessor Prior Aefic of Evesham Abbey had convinced her to found a new Benedictine house for monks in Coventry. This appears to be what she and Leofric did when they changed the nunnery into a house of monks. According to the *Evesham Chronicle:*

Then your worthy Prior Aefic departed from the daylight in the year of Our Lords Incarnation one thousand and thirty eight, and his grave worthily exists in the same church of the Blessed Trinity near that of the same pious Countess Godiva, and of whom, so long as he lived, he was a friend.

Before Godiva died she saw her family connected to the royal family when her grand-daughter Ealdgyth married Harold and became Queen of England. This of course ended abruptly in 1066 when Harold fell at Senlac Hill. Godiva decreed that on her death her jewel rosary should be placed around the neck of the statue of the Virgin in Coventry Priory in the place where her husband and son lay.

Godiva is of course famous for the 'ride'. Whether or not she did it has been a source of debate for centuries. Many people know the story of the famed naked ride or know a version of it. The ride was not actually mentioned until 150 years after Godiva's death. The original tale appears to have been first told by Roger of Wendover in his *Flores Historiarum*. Wendover states:

The Countess Godiva . . . longing to free the town of Coventry from heavy bondage from the oppression of a heavy toll, often with urgent prayers besought her husband . . . he should free the town from that service . . . The earl sharply rebuked her . . . and forbade her ever more to speak to him again on the subject . . . She on the other hand . . . never ceased to exasperate her husband. He at last gave her his answer: Mount your horse and ride naked, before all the people, through the market of the town from one end to the other, and on your return, you shall have your request . . . Whereupon the countess beloved of God, loosened her hair and let down her tresses which covered the whole of her body, like a veil, and then mounting her horse and attended by two knights, she rode through the market place, without being seen, except her fair legs. Having completed the journey, she returned with gladness to her astonished husband and obtained from him what she had asked for . . .

Wendover's work only survives as a fourteenth-century manuscript, so this may not be original. At least two other versions survive, written or revised by Wendover at his scriptorium in St Albans. In one account Leofric isn't astonished but filled with admiration. In another account, most likely the original, Godiva rode through the marketplace seen by no one and Leofric declared it a miracle. This miracle is later repeated in an account written by Matthew of Westminster. In the *Chronica Majora* written in the early thirteenth century Matthew Paris described it as 'hoc pro miraculo'. The earliest sources in general go along with a miracle taking place: Godiva had ridden through the marketplace accompanied by two knights and nobody saw her. No one can of course claim that the act of covering her body with

Sir William Reid Dick, the sculptor, and American ambassador's wife Mrs Lewis Douglas after the unveiling of the Godiva statue in Broadgate in 1949.

her hair was miraculous; possible with lots of very long voluptuous hair but certainly not miraculous. If the lady had however ridden naked through the people and nobody saw her nakedness this would of course imply the intervention of God to save the lady's dignity. This certainly would be a miracle like many other miraculous tales of the time.

It appears that the story of Godiva's ride was probably carried to St Albans by monks who were cast out of the priory in 1190 for trying to kill the bishop, Hugh de Nonant, by splitting his skull with a crucifix before the high altar. This tale of self-sacrifice may have been linked onto an ancient fertility procession. At Southam (20 miles from Coventry) which also belonged to Leofric and Godiva the villagers had a Godiva procession which lasted up until about 1848. In this Godiva procession there were two woman on horseback, one black, one white, called the 'Black and White Lady' draped over with lace (like the older Coventry Godivas), making them virtually invisible. They were led through the village by a man wearing a horned bull's mask known as 'Brazen Face'. The black and white lady refers to the two aspects of the goddess and Brazen Face was the Shining One, the sun/fertility god related to the ancient pagan British 'Oosers'. These aspects can be related to ceremonies involving the goddesses Isis and her consort Osiris, both linked to fertility in agriculture, the cults of whom were brought over to England in the Iron Age. Even the use of lace or nets like the early Coventry Godivas can be explained by the Goddess Isis. Apparently Isis had the ability to cast a mist of invisibility around her, 'So no man can see where or whence I go.' Hence the goddess passes through the people unseen, a miracle!

GODIVA PROCESSION

The city annals of 1678 state:

> *31 May 1678 being the Great Fair at Coventry there was an extraordinary Divers of Companies – set out each a follower. The Mayor and the Sheriffs each one and two at the publick charge, there were divers Streamers with the Companies arms and Ja. Swinnertons Son represented Godiva.*

The casualness of this entry gives the impression that James Swinnerton's son may not have been the first Godiva impersonator. The reason for mentioning this particular ride may be that James Swinnerton himself was well known in the city. This is backed up by another version of the annals which states, for 1678: 'Godiva ride, commonly known and yearly commemorated by the Mayor, Alderman and ye several companies.' It is highly possible that earlier processions may have been linked onto the already existing St George procession known as the 'Riding of the George'. In fact St George continued to be the figure leading the early Godiva processions. The first recorded boy playing Godiva was certainly added to the Great Show Fair of 1678 which began with a great procession led by the mayor and city alderman. The procession of 1710 was the first which was attended by men wearing the pikeman's armour from St Mary's Hall. It was said of the June 1789 procession that 'a most enchanting GODIVA will grace the buly scene, mounted on a white steed; the overcurious Peeping Tom is hourly expected to disappear and be new clothed, that he may be ready to reassume his ancient post'. It was traditional for Peeping Tom to be dressed for the occasion.

The Godiva procession of June 1824 was described thus:

> *The bells rang most harmoniously during the whole of the day; the towers, battlements of the churches were thronged with spectators, and the streets were nearly rendered impassable . . . At eleven o'clock, the Mayor, Magistrates, and Charter Officers, attended divine service . . . at half past 12, the procession moved forward, and having passed through all the principal streets, terminated at four o'clock . . . The fair Godiva was never personified by a female who looked more lovely . . . St George, in black. – and the Knight in polished armour, added dignity to the scene . . . the cavalcade was of an unusual extent, owing to the increased number of followers introduced by the Societies.*

In 1845 many notable local citizens and clergy tried to get the procession stopped. The bishop of Worcester wrote to William Clark, who was then mayor, stating:

> *My attention has been called to a custom which I am told prevails in Coventry every third year, and which is so offensive to every right feeling that I could not have believed it to have been permitted in a civilised and Christian country . . . It is stated to me, that every third year a common prostitute is hired at Birmingham, for the purpose of being paraded through the streets of Coventry, as a representative of Queen Godiva. That the said prostitute is dressed in a tight fitting dress of flesh colour, so as to give her the appearance of being naked, and is of course followed by a mob of the lowest rabble in Coventry.*

Despite this and other attacks, the procession of May 1845 went ahead, with the Godiva dressing in the home of Mr Bird the chemist in Earl Street and not in St Mary's Hall as was usual. The lady in question could have offended few for she wore a tight flesh coloured dress over which she wore a tunic of white satin, edged with gold lace and a girdle of the same material. Across her shoulders were two blonde coloured scarves, with a blonde-coloured polka dot mantle with sleeves all decorated with butterflies and leaves. She also wore a wig with tiara and a plume of ostrich feathers. The procession started from the courtyard of St Mary's Hall and tens of thousands lined the route, but the event was spoilt by torrential rain which effectively made the procession speed up in desperation to get back under cover, thereby missing

La Milo rides through a packed Broadgate in 1907.

some parts of the route. Greyfriars Green, it was said, was turned into a sea of mud, four inches deep.

Attitudes amongst the clergy didn't change much, for in 1907, as Pansy Montague known as La Milo rode free for charity as Godiva before 100,000 people, Canon Beaumont described her attire as 'unspeakably vulgar'. The Revd Brodie of Christchurch called the ride 'sensual and devilish'. Others called it an outrage, disgusting and a disgrace to the city. Others just enjoyed it for what it was. With the coming of the Great War the next procession wasn't until 1919 when Gladys Mann rode as the lady, this time wearing full Saxon regalia. This procession took place at a time when lots of servicemen were returning from war and, because of lack of work, many cities around the land had witnessed riots. After a successful procession all seemed well until a small group of men decided to attack shops in Broadgate, claiming they were German owned. This sparked a full-blown riot, with hundreds fighting police in the streets. Broadgate was badly damaged before the police managed to bring the event under control.

The 1936 procession was a more sedate affair, with 22-year-old Birmingham girl Frances Burchell riding as Godiva. The event was used to raise money for the Coventry and Warwickshire Hospital and it was estimated that 200,000 people lined the processional route and 100,000 attended the fair afterwards in the Memorial Park. Frances Burchell said after the event, 'Tell them I enjoyed every minute of the ride, and the public response was marvellous. What impressed me most was the way the men bared their heads. The amount of reverence and respect that was shown was awe inspiring.' The procession still survives today but is now a much smaller event taking place in June.

GOSFORD GREEN

Gosford Green has been a piece of open land for centuries. Here in 1398 John Mowbray, duke of Norfolk, and Henry Bolingbroke, duke of Hereford, faced each other in a combat to the death before Richard II. Hereford had branded Norfolk a traitor and soon both men accused each other of the same charge. It went to Parliament and before the sitting Hereford added further accusations, saying Norfolk was responsible for the murder of his uncle, the duke of Gloucester. Parliament decided that Hereford could not prove his case, unless he proved it by trial by combat. At a second meeting it was decided that the two men should prove their case on Gosford Green on 17 September 1398. Both men made preparations for the event, Hereford had a new suit of armour made by the royal armourers in Milan and Norfolk's was made by armourers in Germany. Norfolk stayed at Caludon Castle and Hereford stayed at Baginton Castle. The great day arrived and thousands poured into Coventry. Both men mounted their beautifully dressed horses in their brand-new armour ready to prove their cause, but King Richard

Richard II stops Norfolk and Hereford on Gosford Green.

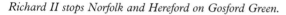

stopped the event at the beginning and both men were exiled. Henry Bolingbroke later returned to England and took Richard's throne, crowning himself King Henry IV.

In 1469 Earl Rivers and his son, the father and brother of Elizabeth Woodville, queen of Edward IV, were beheaded here by order of the earl of Warwick. On 29 March 1471 Edward IV arrived with an army of 30,000 and camped on the green as he waited for the earl of Warwick to meet him in battle. The earl refused. Edward arrived again on 5 April with a larger army and again Warwick refused to meet him in battle.

In the 1860s the end of the green nearest the city was an almost circular piece of land known as 'Tithe Barn Piece'. Here in the recent past stood an old tithe barn by the chapel of St Margaret. It was later used as a plant nursery. The green above it consisted of undulating ground with hollows and humps, with a flat area in the centre. In November 1882 the area was acquired by the council as an extension to the green to improve it as a recreation area.

In 1885–6 during a period of high unemployment men were given work levelling the green, filling in hollows and removing humps, one of which turned out to be an undisturbed medieval dump. In 1887 work was under way to widen the lower end of St Michael's churchyard. From here 150 loads of earth were removed and dumped along the Binley Road side of the green. It was said at the time that every load was full of bones so future historians finding them would believe an ancient battle took place here!

GREAT FLOOD

The centre of Coventry was once a great natural lake which probably grew and shrank depending on the season. Sometimes in exceptional circumstances floods happened, filling the low-lying areas of the city. The earliest recorded flood in the city centre is mentioned in *Stowe's Chronicles* under the date of 1607:

> *The cittie of Coventrie is situated upon the mount or rising of a small hill, upon which place there arose a most strange and dreadfull sodaine inundation, the manner whereof followeth, word for word, as I received it under the seale of the citty, and signed by Henrie Sewell, Maior of Coventry: 'Know ye, that we aswel of our owne knowledge as of the credible report of our honest neighbours, Cittizens of Coventry, who have sustained great losses lately by a sudden floud, which unexpected and suddenly came first into the Suburbes of the Cittie.*

> *From whence or where the rayne that caused that sodaine floud came, we know not, but uppon Fryday morning, being the 17th of April, 1607, about seaven of the cloake, no man suspected any such floud to be, and suddenly between eyght and nine of the clock that morning, there was a great floud coming towards the*

The bottom of Smithford Street, Fleet Street and West Orchard under water in 1900 filling the natural area of the ancient Babbu Lacu.

Cittie whereupon some seeing it come halfe a myle off and made it knowne unto some citizens to make present hast to save some of their goods, but the water came so abundantly, like the surges of the sea, into the Suburbes and Citty, that it rose within one houre in some places three yards and better in height.

More than it was that morning and overflowed divers meadows, and grounds, and entered through the streets and houses of the Inhabitantes that dwelt neere the river to the number of two hundredth, fiftee, and seven houses, besides worke houses, and other houses of office, neere the river, to the hurt of Tanners, Whittawers, Dyers, Bakers and Bruers. Not only in their householde goods, but in carrying away many things, to their great losse and damage.

Another notable flood was on New Year's Eve 1900 when the Sherbourne and Radford Brook burst their banks, flooding Spon Street, Hill Street, Queen Victoria Road and Smithford Street. St John the Baptist church still has a marker on the inside wall recalling the event and marking the water depth in the building as being 5 feet. The *Midland Daily Telegraph* reported the following day:

West Orchard was the first locality visited . . . in two of the houses which stand nearest the Sherbourne the rising torrent had actually burst in the walls of the rooms on the ground floor and made a clean sweep of everything – furniture, ornaments, kitchen utensils, food, clothes – absolutely everything. Even the paper was partly torn from the walls . . .

Only one man died. Joseph Sheward, a deaf 64-year-old man living in a downstairs room in Hill Street was trapped for over two hours, naked and up to his neck in freezing water, and although a neighbour tried to rescue him the conditions proved too hazardous and the old man died of cold and shock.

GUILD CHAIR

Standing in St Mary's Hall is one of the best surviving medieval chairs in England, which for the past 150 years has often been referred to as the 'Guild Chair'. It has been suggested that it was a double chair shared by the master of the Trinity Guild and the mayor. This would be either in the sense that the two ennobled figures were squeezed onto the chair or perhaps the chair was attached to another seat. This can only be partly true, as it has an attachment for a screen, but not a seat. Whoever came up with this story probably also dated the chair to 1450, simply because they linked the two lions on the uppermost part of the chair to Edward IV, thus giving the date. Here the story also falls apart, for Henry VI was king in 1450.

In reality precedence states that Coventry's mayor was always followed by the city recorder, then the master of the guild (except for one short instance), so the two men never shared a chair. In fact the only chair-sharing was when the incoming and outgoing mayors shared a bench during mayor making. As for the so-called 'Guild Chair', it actually belongs to the decorated period of 1272–1380 and not the perpendicular of the fifteenth century. It has double arches and quarter foils, which places this chair in the mid to late fourteenth century. The chair is not recorded as being in the hall when an inventory was taken in 1441. Its first appearance there was actually recorded in 1579 when 6 pence was paid to bring it from the old Corpus Christi Hall.

Clues on the 'Guild Chair' tell of its real origins. It has the grape vine representing the blood of Christ, the three acorns representing the Trinity and the three roses representing the fifteen mysteries of the Catholic faith. It also has hunting scenes including a huntsman and his dog and two hunting dogs pinning down an unknown animal, also a huntsman pinning down a deer. The chair blends Christian symbolism

The Great Chair in St Mary's Hall.

with hunting. Hunting in association with Christian symbolism isn't unusual and was also found decorating the Pilgrim's Rest, the priory guest house in Palmer Lane. This gives a clue to the chair's origin and places it where many eighteenth-century writers thought it came from: the choir in Coventry's priory cathedral of St Mary. The 'Guild Chair' called the 'Great Chair' from its first appearance in the hall is in fact most likely the throne of Coventry's ancient bishops or priors or both.

To add backing to this, the chair still has the lugs on its back to take the metal-framed canopy which would have covered the head of the bishop/prior and the holes survive for the bottom board so that his feet would not touch the ground. On its side can be seen the fittings where it could have been attached to the choir stall and the two figures on either side of the chair are the elephant and castle for Coventry and the double lion holding the now removed mitre for the bishop of Lichfield. The top of the mitre has been chiselled off. This could also relate to one of the church's priors. Lastly, on the side of the chair, large but tucked away, is the Virgin seated holding Christ: the seal of Coventry Priory.

☞ *See* **ST MARY'S HALL**

GUILDS

A guild consists of a group of individuals who share either business or trade interests. Originally set up for charitable purposes, guilds quickly became self-contained groups whose interest was mainly based around themselves. They protected each other financially and mortally through maintaining churches and chantries. They also protected their trades and businesses by controlling who was allowed to trade and work in the city. Coventry's first guild was the merchant guild of St Mary founded in 1340. This guild was responsible for the origins of St Mary's Hall. Between 1364 and 1369 St Mary's Guild amalgamated with the guild of John the Baptist (founded 1343), St Catherine (founded 1343) and the Trinity Guild (founded 1364). Their union was confirmed in 1392 and the guild was known as the Guild of the Holy Trinity, St Mary, St John the Baptist and St Catherine. This was quickly shortened to simply the Guild of the Holy Trinity or Trinity Guild.

The Trinity Guild controlled trade in the city and counted amongst its members kings and noble families. Those who joined the Trinity Guild also had cheap quayage at Bristol docks, which was a definite advantage as Coventry merchants traded throughout Europe. Being the most powerful men in the city they also formed the council and those who were masters of the guild afterwards became mayors of Coventry. The merchant guilds were dissolved in 1547 by an Act of King Edward VI and the guildhall was confiscated by the Crown. Shortly before it was dissolved the now falling membership of the Trinity Guild was joined by Coventry's other merchant guild, the guild of Corpus Christi, who maintained Corpus Christi Hall and St Nicholas's Church in Radford.

Coventry's second group of guilds was the trade or craft guilds. These were originally suppressed by the merchant guilds but later allowed to form. The members of these guilds had to serve an apprenticeship to practise their craft in the city and also follow the guild's regulations. Masters took on a limited number of apprentices who taught them the trade for seven years and the apprentice was then made a freeman. Afterwards these craftsmen became journeymen who could work for anyone. If the journeyman wished to become a master and set up in business by himself he would then apply to the guild of his trade for permission and would then be expected to take on apprentices himself, thus maintaining the quality of the trade in the city. The trades included such occupations as weavers, drapers, smiths, tailors, shearmen and mercers, to name but a few. These guilds maintained chapels in Coventry's various churches.

In times of war the trade guilds had to supply the monarch with men who had trained in the use of weapons. The trade guilds also maintained and played parts in the Mystery Plays for which Coventry was once famous.

H

HALES, JOHN

John Hales was the younger son of Thomas Hales, born at Hales Place, Halden. He carried the nickname 'club foot' because as a youth he accidentally dropped a dagger which pierced and damaged his foot, giving him a life-long limp. Hales was educated at Oxford, where he became proficient in Latin, Greek and Hebrew. He also became well versed in antiquities and the law.

In the reign of Henry VIII he was made clerk of the hanaper and acquired a baronetcy. His love of property speculation grew with the Dissolution of the Monasteries when he acquired many properties and land in Warwickshire and other counties. Many of these he sold on to make a further profit. Hales acquired and sold on Coventry Priory but kept Whitefriars to himself, turning it into a house he called 'Hales Place'. He is credited with founding the Free or Grammar School in the city, but he actually founded it on the wishes of the King. In fact while Hales was in London he enquired from the King about purchasing property in Coventry and Henry made it clear that he would show willing if the purchaser opened a grammar school in the city.

Hales did as the King wished and founded a grammar school within the old Whitefriars church, but showed little interest in it, paying only a minimum yearly stipend for its upkeep. The King also gave Hales land towards the school's upkeep, but this was never used for the school's benefit and Hales kept it for himself. When Queen Elizabeth visited, the city recorder John Throckmorton in a speech to her gave vent to the city's anger on the subject.

It seems that the city fathers believed Hales was going to found a school in his own property but Hales had no such intention and instead asked the corporation if he could use the disused Whitefriars church behind his property. The council gave permission but as Hales had no intention of supporting the school properly it was closed and the building repossessed. After many attacks on him, Hales later set up the school again in the old chapel of St John and in 1572 left property and land to pay for its upkeep. After his death the document was found to be invalid and it was written: 'the godly purpose of the said John Hales may be hereafter called into question and utterly overthrown'.

Although Hales has come down to us with a good reputation, few in his time would have recognized this, as Leland wrote: 'Hales with the clubbe foot, hath gotten an Interest in this Colledge, and none can get him out.' A phrase was added into the sentence as an afterthought, saying none 'but the

John Hales, property speculator and 'founder' of the Grammar School.

devil' can get him out. Hales obviously had a reputation and no doubt much of it was due to the fact that he appeared to have come to Coventry to speculate and make cash on the back of the Dissolution, for Hales acquired during this period many monastic buildings and estates, including the priory itself, St John's and of course Whitefriars, which he converted into a second home.

Hales caused controversy in more than one way in his time in Coventry for in 1560 he was believed to be involved with the printing of seditious documents known as the Martin Marprelate Tracts at Whitefriars itself. Hales himself claimed to have no knowledge of the affair and to have been living elsewhere when the offence took place. His guilt was still suspected and he was fined £1,500, which he managed to get reduced to only £500. Despite this he still ended up in the Tower for a short time, but had been forgiven his offence by the time Queen Elizabeth stayed at Hales Place in 1565.

John Hales died at his other 'Hales Place' in London on 28 December 1572 and was buried near there in the church of St Peter. He died without issue and his estate was passed on to his nephew, also called John Hales.

HARFORD, JOHN

John Harford was mayor of Coventry in 1569 and is the only Coventry mayor to hold the dubious title of 'murderer'. John Harford was walking his two greyhounds in the fields when he came upon a certain William Heeley, who was out walking his spaniel accompanied by his wife and mother. All was well until suddenly Harford's greyhounds attacked the spaniel and William Heeley tried to beat them off. Enraged, Harford ran at him and struck him a number of violent blows with his walking staff across the back. Heeley survived the attack, but suffered two weeks of pain before dying. At Heeley's inquest Coventry's mayor John Harford was found guilty of manslaughter and Queen Elizabeth herself ordered his removal from office. John Harford did not, however, suffer unduly for his actions as William Heeley's widow accepted an unspecified sum of money to drop the prosecution.

HARINGTON, SIR JOHN

Sir John Harington of Exton in Rutlandshire was also lord of Coombe Abbey, which stands on the outskirts of the city. It was here that he was visited by King James I who is said to have rushed to London after Elizabeth's death to claim the throne in undue haste, dispensing knighthoods along the way. Apart from a new title he also left the responsibility for the upbringing of his 7-year-old daughter, the Princess Elizabeth, to Harington, with a promise that he would pay towards her upkeep, a promise which he never kept.

The princess was educated with other young noble ladies at Coombe, which he turned into a wonderland with menageries and miniature cattle and horses. While here she made her first official visit to Coventry accompanied by Lord Harington. The princess feasted at St Mary's Hall and was presented with the traditional Coventry Cup three-quarters of a yard high which was so tall that she had to be assisted by Lord Harington.

On 5 November 1605 the Gunpowder Plot was hatched and a large group of Catholics gathered on Dunsmore Heath in the guise of a hunting party, planning after the royal assassination to ride on Coombe, take the princess and marry her to a Catholic peer and run England through her. Harington heard of the gathering and quickly moved the princess to the safety of walled Coventry and there she remained while the threat was current. The upkeep of the princess did profound damage to Harington's coffers and, although James offered him the right to strike a farthing, Harington never took up the offer and died virtually bankrupt in Worms.

Sir John Harington of Coombe Abbey, protector of the Princess Elizabeth.

HARRIS, MARY DORMER

Mary Dormer Harris, a farmer's daughter, was born at Dale House Farm, Stoneleigh, in 1867. She attended school in nearby Kenilworth until her father's death in 1882 when she moved to London to stay with relatives. There she attended the Richmond and Twickenham High School for Young Ladies and when she was 18 she won a place of Oxford University. In 1888 she obtained a first class degree in English, being only the second student in her college to obtain the pass. Mary then took up a teaching post. In 1896 her mother needed her help so Mary returned to Warwickshire and lived in Leamington Spa. At this time she returned to her life-long interest in Coventry's past, writing a paper on the city's craft guilds. This was read for her before the Society of Antiquarians as women were not allowed.

In 1898 her first book about Coventry was published: *Life in an Old English Town*. From this time Mary's reputation as a writer and lecturer grew. In 1904 she began her translation of Coventry's massive Leet Book, a task which would take her ten years. At the end of 1906 Mary and her mother moved into 16 Gaveston Road, Leamington, where she would live for the next thirty years. The Leet Book was published in four sections between 1907 and 1913 and remained an invaluable resource for historians.

In 1911 Mary's book, *The Story of Coventry*, was published, a revamp of her 1898 book. In 1914 she and a number of other prominent Coventry citizens founded the Coventry Guild, a society sworn to protect Coventry's ancient architecture and also to found a city museum. One important building under threat at this time was Palace Yard, which thanks to the Coventry Guild survived and was restored, ironically to be destroyed in the Second World War.

The year 1924 saw the publication of perhaps her most popular work, *Unknown Warwickshire*, and from this time she regularly contributed to the Coventry newspapers. She wrote of Coventry at this time, 'The more I write of Coventry the less I am able to put into words the spell it casts over those who love it. In this wonderful place the old and the new are inextricably mixed together . . .'

Mary Dormer Harris as a young woman.

She worked as a lecturer in Birmingham University, continued writing and appeared on the new-fangled radio. During this time in 1925 she saved the Stoneleigh mummers' play for prosperity by recording it and it is now played in the village every year. Mary was even a founder member of the Loft Theatre in Leamington. Her sense of fun and humour shone through she wrote late in her career: 'A dull book of mine has just come out . . . about two people seem to like it; or at least they tell me so'.

On a quiet evening on 2 March 1926 Mary Dormer Harris was crossing the Rugby Road in Leamington when she was hit by a car and instantly killed. She carried no handbag and her body wasn't identified until the following morning. Having spent decades studying ancient manuscripts her eyesight was very poor so she may not have seen the vehicle approaching her. Alternatively she may have been deep in thought over some historical conundrum. A sad end to a wonderful career.

HENRY VI

The most important king linked to Coventry was Henry VI; his first visit to the city was on the 12 June 1434 when he received a silver gilt cup. Henry visited again in 1437 and spent that Christmas in nearby Kenilworth Castle.

In June 1450 the rebel Jack Cade led a large force of armed men on the capital, forcing the royal household to flee to the safety of walled Coventry. The King was again in Coventry on 21 September 1451 when he stayed at the priory and held a royal procession to celebrate high mass in St Michael's church. The Leet Book recalls the event:

> *the mayor and his peers clad in scarlet gowns with their cloaks, and all other in their scarlet gowns, went unto the King's chamber door . . . The mayor then and his peers doing to the King due observance when he came from his chamber, took his mace and bore it before the King and all his brethren . . . till he got to St Michaels and brought the King to his closet. There the said bishop [Beaufort] in his pontificals . . . with all the Priests and Clerks went in procession around the churchyard. The King devotedly, with many other lords followed the said procession bare headed, clad in a gown of gold tissue, furred with a fur of martin sable . . .*

After mass Henry returned to his room in the priory and sent the gown he had worn as a gift to the church. The king left and was accompanied to Astill Grove by the lane to Canley by the mayor and his brethren. Henry spoke, 'Sirs, I thank you of your good rule and demesne at this time, and for good rule among you, before had and in special for your good rule of this year last past.' Henry then declared that Coventry would become its own county.

In 1455 the duke of York was threatening the crown and Henry again moved to the safety of Coventry. In 1456 Henry's life was under threat in London and the entire royal court moved to Coventry and in December of that year the Royal Jewel House followed. From this date, for over two and a half years, Coventry effectively became the seat of royal power and Henry and Margaret

Henry VI, king and saint.

processed from the city, using it as their base. During a two-month stay in 1459 the entire royal army camped outside, awaiting the Queen's pleasure. A Great Council was held in the priory in which many Yorkist lords were denounced as traitors. This was later followed by a sitting of Parliament, again in the priory. This became known as the *Parliamentum Diabolicum* or the

'Parliament of Devils'. Here thirty-two Yorkist lords were attainted, outlawed and their goods seized by the crown.

The Yorkist swore to get the Act reversed, if necessary by force of arms, and in June 1460, while the Yorkists flocked to Warwick's standard, King Henry himself made a call to arms in Coventry. At the beginning of July he left the city for the last time, leaving Margaret and Edward behind, and met with the Yorkist army at Northampton. Henry was defeated by Warwick and was escorted back to London while Margaret and Edward fled to Wales.

After more battles Henry was deposed by the earl of March who was declared King Edward IV. After the Battle of Towton Henry fled north, pursued by Warwick. Things did not go as the earl of Warwick planned so he changed sides and released Henry from his confinement in the Tower. Warwick was killed at Barnet and shortly afterwards Henry's son, Prince Edward, was killed after the Battle of Tewkesbury. Margaret was brought back to the city and stood before Edward IV, a prisoner. She rained down curses upon him and Edward, although tempted, drew back from having her executed. Within days Edward and Margaret were back in London and no sooner had they arrived in the capital than Henry was murdered in the Tower.

Henry's body was put on public display and bled before the people, proving to all that he had been murdered. His body was then interred in Chertsey Abbey. Soon miracles were claimed and thus began one of the greatest cults in England.

☛ *See* **COVENTRY TAPESTRY**

HEWITT, JOHN

Alderman John Hewitt Junior was probably Coventry's most outstanding mayor; he was the son of John Hewitt, a silk man who was mayor in 1750. Hewitt also a silk man was first made mayor of Coventry in 1755. For his inauguration he held a spectacular feast at St Mary's Hall. Hewitt was re-elected to the office of mayor another two times. He was also a justice of the peace and magistrate and in this role actively fought crime throughout his thirty-year career. Hewitt was a first-class thief-taker, with connections to the other great thief-taker in London, Sir John Fielding. From the Mayor's Parlour in Cross Cheaping Hewitt fought crime, sending many to the gallows – including in 1763 the Coventry Gang (members of a 200-strong gang of London-based thieves) and the murderers of Stoneleigh farmer Thomas Edwards, who were hanged and gibbeted on Gibbet Hill in 1765.

Hewitt appeared to be a man of great moral fibre and of unswerving loyalty to the people of Coventry. His need to protect the people was paramount and he also showed this part of his character to the villains he captured. The Gibbet Hill murderers received many favours from Hewitt in gaol and were very well treated; Hewitt himself was very upset, as these men stated that they would die happy if they could blow his brains out! Hewitt did not understand how those he treated honourably could turn against him, despite the fact that he wished to hang them!

One of Hewitt's cases involved one of the greatest wood carvers and engravers of the eighteenth century, Thomas Lightowller. The latter with his brothers did work beautifying many stately homes including Warwick Castle. At one point he worked for the empress of Austria for £300 a year, a huge sum in those days. Lightowller also did some work for Hewitt and it was four years later, in 1755, when the solicitor of the Royal Mint asked Hewitt if he could help capture Lightowller who had apparently used his skill to forge coins and banknotes.

Discovering the situation, Hewitt dug into Lightowller's past and found a trail of forgery followed him. Hewitt quickly established that Lightowller was back in Coventry and he made it known that he wanted to speak to him about more wood carving. Through this he found Lightowller's lodgings and, attended by the high constable and a number of officers who thought they were to arrest a soldier, Hewitt went to apprehend him. When asked, the landlord claimed that Lightowller didn't lodge there. Hewitt would have none of it and ordered the landlord to take him to the room. He later wrote of the event:

> *Upon going up the first stairs he wraps gently on the door, as he was taking me up a second storey. Considering the wrap a signal and him a traitor, I immediately collared him, kicked up his heels, and sent him backwards downstairs, and with my foot against the door forced the lock and bolt. The moment I perceived by the clothes Lightowller was in bed I looked back for my attendants. Not one man in sight. Perceiving my danger, and the terror I had put the woman in, I addressed her, 'Mrs Lightowller, don't be surprised; this husband of yours can't leave off his tricks.'*

Hewitt gave Lighthowller the chance to dress, once he had put his pistol back under his pillow. He then quickly alerted his deserting officers and ordered them to bring Lightowller to him. Later items for coin and bank note forging were found in Lighthowller's room. Soon after Lighthowller bribed a guard and escaped, but Hewitt had him retaken for trial. In later life Hewitt recorded many of his major cases in a journal which was published in two parts. Alderman John Hewitt lies buried in the south aisle of Holy Trinity Church, although his resting place can no longer be found.

HINDS

Hinds & Co. was Coventry's premier soft drink company, producing fizzy pop through the nineteenth and early twentieth centuries in a small factory in Hales Street next to the grammar school. The actual business was started by a Mr Walker around 1866 and was soon after sold to James Hinds, whose son John took the business on from strength to strength. The locally famed drinks invented by John and his father were registered to the firm and included such strange concoctions as 'phosphorzine', described in 1896 as being 'a great brain, nerve and constitutional invigorator'. Another unusual drink was 'quinazine', said to aid those who suffered from indigestion. Two of the firm's favourites were Godiva and Peeping Tom Ginger ale. These were just a few of the thirty soft drinks produced by the company. John Hinds was justifiably proud of his products and looked over the process from his office. His 'factory' was reputed to be meticulously clean. The water John used was said to be beyond pure and probably came from the same source that once fed St Agnes's Well in St Agnes Lane. This water was noted for its purity, yet John Hinds had it double filtered before use in an expensive modern filtration system, thickly lined with silver so that the water would remain untainted.

Hinds drinks were sold in ordinary bottles, marbled stoppered bottles and siphon bottles, all of which were decorated with Coventry's elephant and castle. He not only supplied the city but also sent carts out for a 20 mile radius. Other bottles travelled further, being shipped abroad to the colonies. In 1896 Granville Sharp, a chemical analyst, wrote: 'I am in a position to form a very favourable opinion as to the skill and care that has been brought to bear in their preparation, as they are free from pollution, palatable and wholesome.'

HIPPODROME

Coventry's first Hippodrome theatre opened in 1884 and was a corrugated iron and wooden building which stood in Pool Meadow. This was replaced by a new building in Hales Street in 1906. This building saw many greats, such as Charlie Chaplin, Harry Lauder and George Robey. In December 1936 work began on a 'new' Hippodrome. This new Art Deco building was constructed using 550 tons of massive steel girders made by Boulton & Paul. Three and a half million bricks were used to face the building and more than twenty miles of cable. The building took 200 workmen ten months to build. Most of the interior of the building was designed by top Deco studio Bath Artcraft who were more used to creating interiors for ocean liners, such as the *Queen Mary*. The theatre had one of the largest stages in the country and could seat 2,000 with 500 standing.

The theatre was run by Sam Newsome, known as Mr Coventry Hippodrome, and it contained a BBC studio for the Coventry Hippodrome Orchestra led by Bill Pethers – which had played on world radio 450 times even before its first performance in the new building. While the new Hippodrome was being constructed the old building stood alongside and played its last show on 31 October 1937. On the next day the new theatre opened. From these small beginnings the Hippodrome hosted many of the nation's greatest stars including Laurel and Hardy, Max Miller, George Formby, Morecambe and Wise (who formed their partnership in Coventry) and others such as Jimmy Hendrix and the Rolling Stones. The Hippodrome later became the Coventry Theatre and ended its days as a bingo hall, being demolished to make way for Millennium Square.

HOB'S HOLE

At the bottom of Cox Street could once be found a pure spring-fed pool called Hob's Hole. This small piece of water appears to have been very important in the past and it was always looked after, even being paved around a few centuries ago. Every year a ceremony took place in which a person would be elected Mayor of Hob's Hole. This unfortunate was cheered and carried shoulder high to the pool then unceremoniously thrown in. Why this happened is forgotten in the mists of time but it can be directly linked to the Celtic belief in making sacrifices into the water. As the water was the entrance to the other world the victim/sacrifice was drowned in the water and sent straight to the gods. The implication of this is that Hob's Hole was originally considered sacred and may of course have received other offerings thrown into it to the gods, such as coins and ritually bent pins, brooches and even possibly swords. It would have been named Hob's Hole as a deliberate act to counteract its pre-Christian sacredness, since this means the Devil's or Demon's Hole. The medieval writer Adam of Bremen described a sacred pool beside an ash tree in Uppsala, Sweden, where sacrifices were performed and a living man was plunged in the water.

HOLLAND, PHILEMON

Doctor Philemon Holland was born in Chelmsford, the son of a divine. He studied at Trinity College, Cambridge, gaining a degree in medicine. He later took an MA at Oxford. He moved to Coventry around 1587–9, where he practised medicine. He moved into a house on the corner of Bishop and Silver Street, next to the grammar school, around 1595. He would later become the master of the school from 1628. In Coventry Holland began his life-long work of translating the classics and many of his translations are still used today. In 1600 he translated Livy and in 1601 Pliny's *Natural History*. In 1603 he completed Plutarch's *Morals* and in 1605 his translation of *Suetonius* was completed. In 1609 he dedicated his

Doctor Philemon Holland, the Translator General.

Ammianus Marcellinus to the mayor and aldermen of Coventry. In that same year the council granted him a lease for twenty-one years on his house.

In 1610 he produced his greatest work, a translation of Camden's *Britannia*. Holland was made a freeman in 1612 and made a long oration to King James I on his visit in 1617. He was made master of the grammar school when 77 years of age and held the post for fourteen months, although he may have previously held the post of usher for twenty years. It is believed that he left the master's post early because it was said he had 'grown weak and decayed'. Despite this, in the same year (1632) his translation of Xenophon's *Cyrupaedia* was published. The corporation, knowing his difficulties, gave Holland a yearly sum of £3 6s 8d, 'for three yeres if he shall so long live'.

Holland grew more impoverished and ill and was now permanently confined to his bed. The master of Magdalene College at this time promised him 'charitable benevolence'. On 9 February 1636 Doctor Philemon Holland, the translator general, died. He was buried in Holy Trinity under an epitaph written by himself, 'I was all earth [Holland = whole land] and all earth I shall be.'

See **OLD GRAMMAR SCHOOL**

HOLY TRINITY CHURCH

Holy Trinity began life as a church attached to Coventry Priory and effectively kept many worshippers out of St Mary's, which was more exclusive. Although we have no actual establishment date for this church, its earliest mention is 1139 and was most likely in existence in the Saxon period. This is backed by the fact that in 1391 the church's chancel was said to be 'ruinated and decayed'. It is very possible that Holy Trinity was Coventry's parish church, for in those early days the chapel of St Michael within the castle bailey was not always accessible. Interestingly in 1218 the Great Fair Charter was fixed at the festival of Holy Trinity and not St Michael. The church also significantly held the curfew bell, a custom usually attached to the parish church. Also many early documents mention St Mary's, St Michael's and the 'parish church', which can only be Trinity.

Trinity held within its walls numerous chapels and chantries. In 1392 Corpus Christi Guild paid for a priest to sing mass in one of the side chapels for the good estate of the king and realm. Many of the priests within the church were supported by the city's various trade guilds and some were supported by land or property left to the church by various individuals. In 1435 to 1460 the church, prompted it is thought by a minor earthquake, had a huge Doom Painting painted over the chancel arch. This amazing work, recently uncovered and restored, depicts Christ on the throne of heaven surrounded by the twelve apostles. The dead rise from their graves and the

A nineteenth-century engraving of Holy Trinity showing the Doom Painting over the chancel arch.

good are admitted into heaven while the bad are cast down into Hell's Mouth by grinning devils. Apart from its nationally important painting, Trinity is unusual for the fact that it is only one of three churches in England to have it charnel house intact and full of skulls and bone under the Marler's Chapel, a chapel paid for by Richard Marler, one of the richest merchants in England.

The church is the last resting place of almost forgotten Elizabethan poet Bartholomew Griffen and was frequented by the later novelist George Eliot, alias Mary Ann Evans. It was in fact this church that Mary Ann refused to attend when she had her blip in faith and got sent away temporarily by her father Robert Evans. Here also took place the marriage of England's greatest Georgian actress Sarah Siddons in 1773 when she married William Kemble. The vicar at the time, one Joseph Rann, who produced volumes on the works of Shakespeare, didn't actually marry the actress, being replaced by his curate. The ceremony was attended by the whole company who were at the time playing a season at Draper's Hall. Shakespearean scholar Rann wanted nothing to do with a ceremony involving 'common players' – ironic, considering that Siddons became the greatest Shakespearean actress of her time.

All of the church's wall-mounted memorials are now fixed in the Archdeacon's Court, a space where church law was once administered. Some memorials still contain their brasses; one is dedicated to Doctor Philemon Holland, the 'Translator General'. Another a decorative stone tomb set against the wall dates to the late fifteenth century and at some time in its past has had the brasses removed. From the surviving insets we can tell that in the centre was a symbol of the Holy Trinity and on each side is the outline of a kneeling man and his sons and, opposite, a kneeling woman with her daughters. Although the creators of this memorial have never been named it is possible to tell that it belonged to the Throckmorton family (sometimes spelt Throgmorton) because the decoration along the top of the memorial consists of a woman's head (the old word 'Throe' meant woman), followed by a barrel topped with a mulberry. The barrel is a tun and the mulberry is the 'mor' or 'mur' berry. Thus giving the name Thro-mor-tun; Throckmorton, a family with close connections to Trinity in past centuries.
See **PHILEMON HOLLAND**

HORSE RACING

It is generally thought that horse racing began in Coventry Park in 1767; it was however earlier than this for Samuel Bradford's map of Coventry of 1748–9 shows quite clearly a winning post near Harvest Hill on the edge of the park. The first surviving account of Coventry Races in the Great Park was in 1755 when Harmless beat Maggot in the first race. This ended in dispute,

Horse racing in 1845.

with the race eventually being awarded to Maggot. The following day, in a race for hunters, five out of the six horses fell, leaving only Mirza standing to win the race and the purse of £50.

An early surviving race card tells us of a race meeting which took place on Wednesday 12 August 1767 and it may be this card which gave rise to the belief that the first races were in 1767. The first race was for the 'City's Purse' of £50 and the winning horse was Edward Popham's chestnut five year old called Leth, ridden by John South. The second horse was Mr Archer's bay called Honest, ridden by Miles Thistlethwaite, and the third Edward Turner's chestnut, Spot, ridden by Robert Wilson. Another three races took place on Thursday, followed by the last race for the 'Chamberlain's Purse' ridden on Friday. These race days were extended especially to provide a 'season' for the local gentry, which also involved balls in Draper's Hall.

The races in the Great Park proved very popular and were well attended. The race meeting which began on 2 September 1783 was said to have been one of the grandest ever, with many notable lords and ladies in attendance at the races and the evening balls in the Draper's Hall. The official races were held on the Monday and Tuesday but on the Wednesday the weavers and butchers suddenly decided that they would ride against each other for a silver cup. The race was accordingly won by a horse belonging to one of the butchers in the city. This extra race, however, ended tragically when a horse broke away with its rider. The horse ran for an open gate but its exit was blocked so the animal jumped the nearby turnstile, landing upon a 7-year-old girl, who was killed instantly. After this event horse racing was brought to an end in the Great Park.

Racing restarted at Stoke Common on a laid-out mile course just beyond Gosford Green. In the *Coventry Herald*, 7 March 1834 we are informed:

> *The Stoke races may now be considered fairly well established as a festival of the sporting calendar . . . By twelve o'clock a larger concourse of people had assembled than we ever remember to have witnessed in the vicinity of Coventry, supposed to amount to 10,000 including many distinguished personages of the county, and sporting characters of the celebrity.*

Stoke Races held the Craven Trial Stakes, which was a recognized trial for the Derby and became quite a prestigious meeting. Despite this the course closed when racing began in Radford near the Conduit Meadows in 1852. The races of 20 and 21 October 1874 were a notable event with large purses. The stewards of the meeting were the earl of Craven, the earl of Aylesford and Lord Calthorpe and the races consisted of the Craven Stakes, Packington Nursery Plates and the Godiva Plate. One of the jockeys who rode at this meeting was a young Fred Archer, who rode 2,748 winners before his sudden and untimely death. During this particular meeting Archer rode Auina to victory in the Packington Plate and on the following day rode Agar to victory and took a second and third place in the two other races. Racing ended in Coventry in the 1880s, mainly due to the fact that the Jockey Club sought to repress the smaller race courses.

HOSPITAL OF SAINT JOHN

The twelfth-century hospital of St John was founded by the prior of St Mary's, Coventry, to look after poor wayfarers. An inquest which took place in the chapter house of the priory in 1425 tells us something of the rules of the house which came under the order of the knights hospitaller. The inquest stated that the monks of the priory had first claim to the prayers of the hospitallers, also to be remembered were Leofric and Godiva for they had founded the priory from which two of St John's brethren were fed everyday.

The master of the house should be a priest of blameless life. He was required to hold a meeting of his community once a week and punish those who did wrong. Grave offences, however, would be under the jurisdiction of the prior. All had to swear an oath to the prior when joining the order. Divine service was to be held daily and on particular occasions the brothers and sisters should attend the priory dressed in their habit. The master and priests in a super tunic of black or brown with a large black cross on the front and the sisters, a super tunic with a white vest and a mantle or close hood. None of these priests or sisters were to communicate with anyone outside the order unless they were in their habits and the sisters were not to leave the premises without covering themselves with a veil or hood.

In 1522 the Hospital of St John consisted of three priests, three clerks and five sisters and maintained thirty beds for the poor. At that time it was said that thirty poor people were kept in the hospital and sometimes there were more. Slightly later Stow says there were five priests and five sisters who kept ten beds for passengers and the poor, who might stay for two nights and two days.

On 4 March 1544 the Hospital of St John was surrendered to the crown. It was valued at just over £95 and was acquired by John Hales. The chapel of the Hospital of St John was later converted into the grammar school – the most notable master of which was Dr Philemon Holland, the translator general.

HUTT, ARTHUR

Arthur Hutt was the first Coventry-born man to win a Victoria Cross. He was born in Earlsdon in 1889 and as a child lived in Gulson Road and attended Holy Trinity Schools. As an adult he worked for Courtaulds, married and lived at 8 Caludon Road, Stoke. Arthur enlisted in the Royal Warwickshire Territorial Division in 1909 and on the outbreak of the First World War he was sent to France, as were his five brothers.

After more than a year at the front, he was discharged and returned home to his job at Courtaulds. But within three months Arthur, now aged 28, returned to the army. Back in France the Warwicks were advancing on Passchendaele. Colonel Barnett recorded what happened next:

On October 4, south-east of Poelcapelle, during the attack on Terrier Farm, this man took command of and led forward No. 2 Platoon when all officers and NCOs had become casualties. He was held up by a strong enemy post on his right and immediately he himself ran forward in front of the platoon and shot the German officer and three men in the post, causing between 40 and 50 to surrender. Later realising that he had pushed too far beyond his objective, he personally covered the withdrawal by sniping the enemy, killing some and then carried back a badly wounded man and put him under shelter. He organised and consolidated his mission and learning that some wounded men were lying out and likely to become prisoners if left there, in the absence of stretcher bearers, he went out in front and carried four wounded men under heavy fire. He held his post until relieved on the 7/8 Oct.

For his outstanding bravery Arthur Hutt was awarded the nation's highest honour, the Victoria Cross. On 12 January 1918 Arthur came home to a hero's welcome in Coventry: he was met at the station and given a civic reception at the Council House, accompanied by his wife and father. In the evening a reception was given at the Drill Hall and at the end of it Arthur Hutt said: 'All I did was my duty to my King and country.' He was demobbed in 1919 and returned home to his wife and new daughter and his job at Courtaulds. In 1959 Arthur Hutt died at his nephew's home in Sewell Highway and was cremated at Canley Crematorium with full military honours. A year later a Cornish granite memorial was erected to him in the Memorial Park.

The Lord Mayor Alderman Fennell said at the service, 'This is the proudest moment of my Lord Mayoralty – to have the honour of unveiling this memorial to our fellow citizen, Arthur Hutt, the only citizen of Coventry ever to have been awarded the greatest honour for bravery and heroism when fighting for his country.'

I

IRON AGE VILLAGE

In 2002, during the construction of a sports pitch at Warwick University, archaeologists discovered a site which had been occupied since Neolithic times. In the past many worked flints have been found and importantly stone axe heads from the axe factory at Craig Llwyd in North Wales have been discovered, showing that a settlement probably lay close to a prehistoric trading route, probably the ancient Welsh Road which passes nearby.

During continuing archaeological excavation a settlement of roundhouses was unearthed, showing people lived on the site between 100 BC and 100 AD. Seventeen roundhouses were excavated, some of which could have been animal enclosures. Archaeologists had difficulty distinguishing which were which as in the 1960s the land had been graded, resulting in the total removal of the actual floor surfaces. Also unearthed was an Iron Age lamp and fragments of pottery.

Further work has shown that the Iron Age village included a ceremonial area which lay within a massive ramparted and ditched enclosure, fragments of which, along with a Neolithic hollow way, can still be seen. The

A Bronze Age axe head found at Whitley.

roundhouses which were excavated were of a large size, measuring up to 18 metres around. It is believed that, because they were so large, many had public or ceremonial purposes and the burial of votive offerings such as horses' heads and pottery backs this up. Other buildings were used by men who smelted metal, the magicians of the Bronze and Iron Ages. Nearby is a banjo enclosure which also probably has a religious significance and is thought to be likely to contain a 'significant' burial.

Around the site, stretching towards Gibbet Hill, are also remnants of prehistoric barrows, showing that this was once an important prehistoric landscape. It has been suggested that Gibbet Hill Road itself is a prehistoric track, as it passes significant prehistoric structures including a defensive Iron Age enclosure in Tocil Wood, which itself dates back at least 2,000 years. Dr Stephen Hill who excavated the site believes that the inhabitants were driven out by the Romans as there is considerable evidence for later Roman occupation of the site. The university site is up until now Coventry's oldest excavated site within the present city boundary. This site could stretch even further, as in the past an Iron Age enclosure was noted as being in the Riddings in Earlsdon. The future could bring more discoveries as the extensiveness of prehistoric settlement in this area is far greater than previously realized.
See **PREHISTORY**

ISABELLA, QUEEN

After Edward II's murder, by having a red hot poker inserted up his rectum, his Queen Isabella didn't view the body but continued as normal. She stayed at Nottingham until 10 November 1327 then moved to Coventry, staying at Cheylesmore Manor a short time. In the dying months of the same year Isabella and her lover Roger Mortimer gained power and she acquired lands and rights in almost every county in England. On her disgrace in 1330 and the execution of Mortimer, his body was interred at Greyfriars in Coventry. A year after he was laid to rest in Coventry his widow (yes, he was married) got permission to remove his body to Wales. Whether this was done or not is not recorded. Isabella herself was stripped of all her lands and powers and was totally dependent on her son. She was sent into enforced retirement in Castle Rising, where she spent most of the rest of her days. By 1337 she was given a yearly income of £1,500 and limited powers as queen dowager. In her old age she took to wearing in penitence the habit of the Poor Clares. She died in 1358 and was buried in the habit in a Franciscan church at Newgate, London.

Interestingly in the past some claim that King Edward II wasn't actually murdered but was forced to leave the country. The claim has re-emerged recently that when Edward III was campaigning in the Low Countries in 1338 he met a man who claimed to be his father. Edward sent two men-at-arms to bring William Le Galeys (or William the Welshman) to his presence. Significantly this man stayed with the King for three weeks. Later William the Welshman returned to England and became the Queen's 'valet'. He added to her Coventry gift of land at St John's church by giving money for a side aisle; also strangely one Gylot de Galey founded Galey's Chapel in Coventry at the same time.

J

JABET'S ASH

Just a few yards from Marlborough Road on the Binley Road stands a modern descendant of the ancient Jabet's Ash. This tree was presented to the city in 1925 by Henry Whiteman and was claimed to have been grown from stock taken from a descendant of the original tree. That tree, mentioned in the late 1300s as the 'Jabotsasshe', appears to have been a boundary tree with an associated ditch. This tree may have also been used as a gibbet for hanging criminals and thus may have acquired the name gibbet ash. It is also even possible, if we go further back in time, that such an ash could be sacred to Woden and such gibbet ashes gained their names from the fact that criminals were hanged on such trees as a gift to Woden. Woden/Odin was sacrificed to himself, hanged on a tree to gain knowledge and wisdom.

Whatever the tree's origin, it and its descendants remained a landmark for centuries. In 1603 James I's daughter, the Princess Elizabeth, was met under the branches of the great tree as she came to Coventry from Coombe Abbey, returning later from there to the splendour of Coombe.

JAGUAR

Jaguar has been based in Coventry since 1928. It began in a back street in Blackpool when 20-year-old William Lyons who then sold motorbikes teamed up with his neighbour William Walmsley who built and sold sidecars under the name of Swallow Sidecars. With the help of their parents they set up in their first premises trading as the Swallow Sidecar Company. Here they built sidecars but also began to build motorcars on chassis made in Coventry. Business thrived and they quickly moved to bigger premises, having their first major success with the Austin Swallow launched in 1927. Orders grew and grew until the two men decided that they needed a larger highly skilled workforce and greater accessibility to parts and so they relocated to Coventry.

Lyons found a location based on the Whitmore Park Estate and in the winter of 1928 Swallow Sidecars moved here, to premises previously used by White & Poppe's munitions. By the end of the first year Swallow was turning out forty cars a week: the Alvis Swallow, the Fiat Swallow and the Swift Swallow. The company grew, taking over more and more of the site and in 1931 Lyons and Walmsley made a deal with Captain Black of the Standard to supply chassis for their new saloon the SS1 and SS2.

The Jaguar stand at Coventry's transport museum.

These new 'SS' models were the showpiece of that year's Olympia Motor Show in London, winning national acclaim. The SS1 was particularly stunning: black with long bonnet and large headlights. With the success of the SS range Swallow continued to expand on the site. Lyons and Walmsley, however, were having problems and Walmsley agreed to retire. In October 1933 Swallow Sidecars disappeared and the company was renamed SS Cars Limited under the sole control of William Lyons. By 1935 Lyons had built up a highly skilled group of engineers and designers and with his new range wanted to change the name to Jaguar. The SS Jaguar six cylinder saloon was launched in September 1935. This was followed in 1936 by the SS Jaguar Tourer and the SS Jaguar 100. By 1938 distribution was worldwide and 5,000 cars were leaving the factory a year.

With the outbreak of the Second World War SS gained a contract to build bombers and the site once again needed to expand. The contract didn't materialize but the company did however gain a contract to build military sidecars. This was followed by repair work on Whitley bombers and other work building sections of Lancasters, Mosquitoes and Spitfires, to name a few. In 1944 the company decided to change its name to Jaguar Cars Limited, as the SS symbol had through the Nazis become a symbol of terror.

In 1951 because the company was unable to expand any further on the Whitmore Park Estate they moved all production to their former shadow factory in Browns Lane, Brownshill Green. During the 1950s the Jaguar name rose to great heights due to their sweeping the board at Le Mans. The company continued producing cars at the Browns Lane site until 2006. The company's design centre remains at Whitley.

JOPSON'S COVENTRY MERCURY

Coventry's first newspaper was first published by Mr Jopson on 20 July 1741. It consisted of four pages and was sold for 2d a week. The newspaper continued with only slight variations to its name until 1836 when it became the *Coventry Standard*. George Eld, who served as mayor in 1834–5, was editor of the *Standard* for 20 years.

K

KNAVE'S POST

The knave's post is a black oak figure of unknown date which up until 1885 stood in a niche in a building in Much Park Street. Offenders would be tied to carts and whipped from the post to the Mayor's Parlour and back. In the 1880s the figure was removed and placed on a buttress in the kitchen of St

Mary's Hall where it remained into the mid-twentieth century until it was removed to the museum.

It has been suggested in the past that the figure may have originated on a tomb in a church but this seems unlikely. The figure bears a likeness to bog oak which had lain for a long period in a boggy place and could possibly be far more ancient than we know. Apart from the fact that parts of the figure have been recut in the past, it bears a remarkable likeness to a number of Bronze Age carved oak deities found in the bogs of Sweden. These images are thought to represent *genii loci*, local gods, and like the 'Knave' have square blocks at their base.

The Knave's Post fixed to a buttress in the medieval kitchen in St Mary's Hall.

L

LAMMAS RIDING

Lammas Lands, that is, land which was available to freemen to graze cattle from Lammas Day (13 August) till Michaelmas (29 September) could be once found surrounding the city. Other land available from Michaelmas was called Michaelmas Land. The first mention of Lammas rights was in the twelfth century when Walter of Coventry created a charter which stated:

> *I Walter of Coventry have given, and by this charter confirmed to all the Comburgisses of Coventrye Common of all the pasture for all the cattle in all my lands, as well as now of inclosed as [or] otherwise, as heretofore time they had it; to have and to holde to them and their Heires in Fee and Inheritence for ever.*

What Walter was doing was effectively giving the burgesses grazing rights over 2,000 acres from Lammas Day to Lady Day (25 March). This was most useful as it was very difficult to sustain cattle over the winter months with reduced herbage, which created the ancient practice of the 'Blood Month', November, when large numbers of cattle, pigs, etc., were killed, butchered and salted or smoked.

The annual riding of the Lammas Lands was led by the city chamberlains and a number of noted individuals from each city ward. The mass ride was originally a public statement of the freemen's right to their land. By the nineteenth century, however, it began to get out of hand when large groups of unruly individuals joined the ride and eventually it was stopped.

LANGTON, WALTER

Walter Langton, bishop of Coventry and Lichfield, was also lord high treasurer of England and close friend of King Edward I. He was respected by the King but not by the future king who fell foul of Walter for his excessive spending on his favourite Piers Gaveston. In his important position Langton made many enemies, some accused him of murder and he lost his bishopric – until he was eventually cleared in Rome in 1303 and restored. That trip cost him a huge 7,000 florins.

Walter Langton was with King Edward when he died on the borders of Scotland and acted as chief executor of the king's will and custodian of the royal body responsible for bringing it safely back to London. No sooner was the king cold than his son Edward II brought his favourite, Gaveston, back from Ireland where his father had sent him. Walter Langton was intercepted at Waltham and imprisoned at Wallingford, the Tower and York. To add insult to injury Edward II gave Gaveston all of Langton's estates.

Eventually a papal bull was issued and Langton was released, although he was excommunicated for refusing to give evidence against Edward and Gaveston. Shortly after his release Gaveston was taken by the earl of Warwick and beheaded on Blacklow Hill beyond Kenilworth. Having perhaps learnt a lesson Edward II called for Langton's excommunication to be dropped and restored him to his estates and to the office of high treasurer. Langton did much building work at the cathedrals of Lichfield and Coventry. He died in London in 1321 and lies at Lichfield.

The tomb of Walter Langton in Lichfield Cathedral.

LEOFRIC

Aelfwine was Leofric's grandfather. His father was Leofwine who was ealdorman of the Hwicce from 994 to 1023. Leofric's brother Northman was executed in 1017 by Canute, and Northman's son Aethelwine was killed in 1014. Leofric's other brothers were Edwin and Godwin. His nephew Leofwine is likely to have been Abbot Leofwine of St Mary's, Coventry. Leofric did not immediately inherit the title 'hlaford Mrycena' (Lord of the Mercians) after Leofwine's death for it appears that a Viking earl, Eglaf, held the title for a very short time, and may have been Godiva's first husband. Canute quickly learnt that it made good sense to keep a number of Saxon lords in power and with this in mind in 1026 he gave the title to Leofric. Canute may have felt that his execution of Northman earlier would ensure Leofric's allegiance.

A stained-glass image of Leofric and Godiva which used to be in Holy Trinity Church.

Despite everything, Leofric did however become close to Canute and proved a stabilizing power in the land.

After Canute's death a national meeting of the Witan was held and Leofric led other earls in support of Harold Harefoot, while Godwin and the West Saxons supported Hardicanute. The final election fell in favour of Harold. Leofric also supported Harold's successor Edward the Confessor to the throne against the Godwins. Leofric was not the grim lord many modern writers profess him to be. He was noted in the *Vitae Aedwardi Regis* as being 'an excellent man, very devoted to God'. Leofric was so devout, he attended mass twice a day and in his lifetime was considered an uncanonized saint. He even witnessed a miracle, a vision of Christ with Edward the Confessor – certainly not the grim and terrible lord who would allow his wife to demean herself in public. He also refounded the church of Coventry and bestowed it with land for its building and upkeep and he did the same for many other holy houses.

Leofric could be hard if the throne was threatened. One such event happened in Worcester when a revolt began which threatened the stability of the monarchy. Leofric crushed the revolt, nearly razing the town to the ground in the process. Yet he was also known as the 'Peacemaker', for his diplomacy often kept peace in the land. Leofric died at his hall in King's Bromley, Staffs, in 1057. The Anglo Saxon Chronicle says: 'In this same year, on 30 October, earl Leofric passed away. He was very wise in all matters, both religious and secular, that benefited all this nation.' He was brought to Coventry with a huge gift of gold and silver and in great pomp laid to rest within one of the porches of the church of St Mary.

LORD MAYOR

Coventry's first lord mayor as opposed to mayor was Alderman H B W Cresswell. This honour was announced by Buckingham Palace on the eve of the Queen's coronation in June 1953. Discussions with the Home Secretary had been under way with Coventry MPs and councillors since 1946 and the successful conclusion was announced on 2 June thus: 'The Queen, on the recommendation of the Home Secretary, has been graciously pleased to command that, in commemoration of her Majesty's Coronation the chief magistrate, now and for the time being, of the City of Coventry, shall be styled Lord Mayor of Coventry.' Thus Alderman Creswell, a goods clerk, became Coventry's first lord mayor.

☞ *See* **ST MARY'S HALL**

LUNT

The Lunt Roman fort stands on the outskirts of Coventry. It is believed that it was first built at the time of the Boudiccan Revolt in AD69 as a training camp for captured Iceni horses. The fort has a wooden gyrus, the only one known in northern Europe, which is believed to have been used to battle condition horses, by riding them around while soldiers shouted and beat their swords against their shields recreating the sounds of battle. Despite the fact that this large military complex stood in Baginton, up until 1958 it was still thought of as the site of a farm or villa. This changed in 1960 when the defensive ditches were first unearthed.

The fort and its attached settlement continued until AD 80 when the fort was abandoned, probably because Julius Agricola needed the troops for his campaign in the north. Archaeology has proved that the legions returned in the reign of Galinus (253–88) and built features, such as the gateway, which have since been rebuilt. In its latter days the Lunt is believed to have been home to the *cohors equitata*, elite cavalry.

The Gyrus for battle conditioning horses at the Lunt Roman Fort, Baginton.

M

MARTYRS

Early seeds of religious turmoil had been sown in Coventry in the 1380s when John Wycliffe tried to break the hold of the Catholic Church by printing the Bible in English. Lollardism was well established in the city and in the reign of Henry VIII those who followed Wycliffe's beliefs would suffer the hate of the church. Henry visited Coventry in 1510, staying at the priory, and in the same year ten Lollards accused of heresy were forced to carry heavy bundles of faggots thorough the marketplace, symbolic of their deaths by fire. All recanted except Joan Ward, who was burned at the stake in the Park Hollows in the Little Park.

In 1519 another group of heretics came to the church's attention for daring to say their prayers and other commandments in English. For this Thomas Lansdail, Hosea Hawkins, Thomas Wrexham, Robert Hocket and Thomas Bond, all respectable God-fearing people, were burned in the Park. Alice Lansdail was discharged and Robert Silksby escaped. Alice Lansdail after being discharged was searched and found to be carrying the Lord's Prayer and commandments in English and was sent to join the others. Robert Silksby was recaptured two years later and met the same fate in the flaming hollows.

During the following years Henry split from Rome, was excommunicated and declared himself the head of the Church of England. He was later succeeded by his son Edward VI whose uncle the duke of Somerset continued the Reformation. After Edward's death and the few days' reign of Lady Jane Grey, Mary was crowned. Mary however was a Catholic and brought the old faith back. Those who did not agree soon began to suffer. In 1555 Lawrence Saunders, rector of All Hallows, London, but known to the people of Coventry, was burned as a heretic in the park. His crime was that he continued to preach the Protestant faith. Saunders was asked to recant on the way to the stake and replied, 'I do not hold heresies but the doctrine of God, the blessed Gospel of Christ; that I hold and believe, that I have taught and that I will never revoke' He was then sent forth to his death.

The next innocent to suffer was Robert Glover taken from his sick bed in Mancetter and brought prisoner to Coventry Gaol. The man who was actually to be arrested for heresy was his brother John, but he had fled after being warned of the forthcoming arrest by the mayor of Coventry, Richard Hopkins. Glover was brought before the bishop to answer questions such as why he failed to attend church. Glover knew this couldn't be proved and replied that he would not attend 'their church as long as their mass was used'.

The burning of Lawrence Saunders from Foxe's Book of Martyrs, *1555.*

He then asked the bishop to show him one 'jot' in the scripture for the defence of the mass. Glover was accused of being arrogant and returned to gaol. He was then taken to Lichfield and received further interrogations before being declared a heretic and sentenced to burn in Coventry on 19 September 1555.

Persecution of the Glovers didn't end here for the bishop of Coventry and Lichfield ordered a new search for John Glover. He escaped again but this time his wife was taken. Glover hid in the woods but died of an 'ague' afterwards and his body was buried in the churchyard. It was ordered that the body be exhumed and cast into the public highway. This was done but none were able to abide the smell and his body was proclaimed damned and reburied. John Glover was not however allowed to rest for twelve months later it was ordered that his bones be dug up and cast back into the highway to be crushed by horses and wagons.

When the last Glover brother, William, died, the bishop of Coventry and Lichfield ordered that the body of this 'rebel against our holy faith' should not be given a Christian burial and that those who tried to do so would answer at their peril. Eventually William Glover's body was dragged away by horses and buried without rites in a broom field.

Two other Coventry men suffered because of religion. The first was John Carlesse, a weaver who was arrested in 1554. Carlesse, described at the time as 'one of the pleasantest Protestants I have ever met', spent two years in Coventry Gaol with his wife and children. After two years he was sent to London and found guilty of heresy. From here he wrote: 'My friends in Coventry have put the Council in remembrance of me . . . saying, I am more worthy to be burned than any that was burned yet. God's blessing in their hearts for this good report.' Carlesse did, however, cheat the flames by dying in gaol.

The second to suffer was Jocelyn Palmer, the son of a Coventry mayor. University-educated Palmer was originally a Catholic who changed his faith after witnessing the burning of Ridley and Latimer. For this he was made to answer, found guilty and burned at the stake in July 1557. A memorial to those who were martyred in Coventry was erected in 1910 near the Park Hollows. It now stands at the bottom of Little Park Street.

MASON, A E

The once-world-famous novelist A E Mason author of the adventure novel, *The Four Feathers*, and many other novels including *Fire over England* and *The Turnstile* was the Liberal MP for Coventry between the years 1906 and 1910. It was said Mason's election battle in Coventry was a particularly fiery one and his novel *The Turnstile* published in 1912 was based on this election and included a number of character sketches of local citizens, such as Alderman Drinkwater, one of Coventry's most notable mayors. Often accompanying him on his Coventry campaign were Lord Grey and J M Barrie, the creator of Peter Pan. Despite representing Coventry, Mason's political career floundered as he was overtaken by his writing career.

MASSEY-FERGUSON

The firm of Massey-Ferguson was started by Irishman, Harry Ferguson, who in 1946 made an agreement with the Standard Motor Company to set up his works in their shadow factory in Banner Lane. This grew into the world's largest tractor plant, selling the world's best-selling tractor for thirty-one years. The Banner Lane plant was 1.8 million square feet, making it the largest tractor factory in the world. Since production began at Banner Lane in 1946 around three million tractors have left the site. The first and perhaps most famous of all the MF tractors was the TE20 (Tractor England) better known as the 'Little Grey Fergie'. In 1953 Ferguson merged with Massey Harris and became Massey-Ferguson in 1958. In 1994 it was reported that well over one million MF tractors were then currently in use over the world. The factory closed in 2005.

MILL DAM

Originally part of the Bablake which stretched through the central valley of the city, the water is usually associated with the Priory Mill and stretched from Pool Meadow towards the grammar school. The pool which formed Pool Meadow and the Mill Dam must have originally been one and the same but at some point the two became separate sheets of water. In the late 1400s a rumour spread throughout the city that a great treasure had been found in or by the Mill Dam. News even got to the ears of Richard II who sent a commission of inquiry but nothing could be found.

By the Mill Dam once stood an ancient ash tree whose branches drooped down towards the water. The once famous tree was known locally as 'Old Nick's Ash'. Many centuries ago a group of people are said to have got together in the Old Grammar School. They drew a pentangle and magic symbols on the floor and followed rites to summon forth the devil. In a flash of light and sulphur the great horned one appeared, but to their surprise he leapt through the glass window and landed on the old ash. It was said the sheer weight of the evil one strained the branches and forever after they hung down and groaned in the wind. In 1847–8 the Priory Mill was taken down and the Mill Dam drained.

MOTOR CAR

The decline of the cycle trade led to the birth of the motor car industry. The foundation of the industry took place in London in April 1896 when Harry Lawson, creator of the first safety cycle, held the first extraordinary meeting of the British Motor Syndicate. Lawson had acquired millions of pounds from investors who wished to invest in the industry which had taken the continent by storm. Lawson used the cash to buy up patents so that he could take control of the industry. He also bought an old cotton mill in Radford to start the British industry using skilled Coventry workers, mainly from the cycle trade.

In May 1896 he launched the Great Horseless Carriage Company from Motor Mills, a building shared with the Daimler Company and other companies. Around the same time the first motor car was driven in Coventry when the French engineer Bollee drove his 'autocar' up and down Hertford Street. The petroleum-powered machine was described as being like a tandem tricycle which was steered by two front wheels. The mayor, Alderman Loudon, joined Bollee as he drove the vehicle up the Kenilworth Road. Here the vehicle was reported as reaching 20 miles per hour in a second or two! It did however have its drawbacks as it shook and rattled over ruts and sometimes was completely enveloped in the dust it disturbed. This car was not a true British-made car but made to Bollee's instructions. It was the

Francis Baron (left) sits at the tiller of one of two Great Horseless Carriage Company vehicles outside Motor Mills, Radford.

British Motor Syndicate, i.e. Harry Lawson, Henry Sturmey and B. Van Praagh, who brought Bollee to Coventry to demonstrate the machine as they had recently acquired the British rights to build it. Bollee caused a sensation and within a fortnight many orders had been placed with the Great Horseless Carriage Company for the vehicle. As Motor Mills was not ready the construction of the vehicles was to take place at the Humber factory, unfortunately and rather suspiciously, the factory burned down with Bollee's car. The first British-built Bollee was manufactured at the Motette factory behind Spon Street. As the original had been destroyed, engineers had to redesign the machine to British specifications. Lawson's company, the Great Horseless Carriage Company, then continued to build the Bollee autocars in June 1896 at Motor Mills, formerly a cotton mill in Draper's Fields, Radford.

After the abolition of the Red Flag Act, work began on the first legal motor cars. History tends to be vague on these beginnings but in the summer of 1897 Major General Montgomery of Winchester ordered the first Daimler car. The Great Horseless Carriage Company, however, produced a number of cars before the Daimler Company, developing a four-wheeled 'phaeton'. Francis Baron, the works manager, wrote in 1944 that his early work on traction engines had been 'the greatest value to me in designing and building the first Light Locomotives called Motor Cars'. Baron says that in 1896, while Daimler were building their first engines, the GHCC were producing Bollee tri-cars. In 1926 it was stated in the press that a Mr Maude was probably the first owner of an autocar in Coventry, having acquired a Bollee from the GHCC in 1896. In 1928 Baron wrote:

> *In 1897 at the Motor Mills, Coventry, I built the first 'petrol' motor cars in England for the Great Horseless Carriage Company Limited. I supplied one to Lord Iveagh for the use of King George (then the Duke of York). In that year, Mr Oliver Stanton, then cycle instructor to the Prince of Wales (later Edward VII) was sent from Sandringham to Coventry to investigate the use of cars by other members of the Royal Family.*

Baron states that the vehicle made for the duke of York was completed in May to June 1897 and was photographed with him at the tiller in July just before delivery, at least a month or two before the first Daimler was completed. This vehicle was renamed the 'Iveagh Phaeton' and around 700 were made by the GHCC. Photographs of these first cars with Baron at the tiller had previous been thought to be Daimler cars. Baron wrote in *Autocar* magazine in 1935 that the Iveagh Phaeton

> *was one of the first dozen built by me, as works manager . . . I contend that the car I have mentioned, which worked continuously without the slightest hitch, being the first petrol car built in England, contributed as much to the present motor industry as George Stephenson's first locomotive to railway development.*

The GHCC became the Motor Manufacturing Company in the spring of 1898 and continued producing cars, as did the Daimler Company. Francis Baron died in 1947 and was remembered as a charming man with a 'wonderfully accurate memory'. In 1905 the MMC moved to Parkside and the Daimler Company took over the whole of Motor Mills and, unlike many of the early companies, lasted well into the twentieth century. During this period many of the city's cycle firms such as Singer, Swift, Rover, Triumph and Humber started producing motor cars. By 1936 the main motor car producers in the city were Alvis, Armstrong Siddeley, Daimler, Hillman, Humber, Lancaster, Riley, Rover, Singer, Triumph and the Standard.

Within a decade of the birth of the industry 10,000 were employed in the trade in Coventry; by 1972 it had reached over 60,000. As the industry grew so did the company as they swallowed each other one by one. The Rootes group took over the Humber and Hillman companies. Rootes was eventually taken over by Chrysler Motors which was itself taken over by Peugeot-Citroen. Over the years companies closed one after the other until today only LTI taxis are produced in the city. Previously since 1896 there have been 110 different motor car manufacturers in the city.

MYSTERY PLAYS

The mystery play may have derived from dramatizations performed in connection with the church. These events were later taken on by city trade guilds in York, Chester and Coventry. These three cities are the most famed home to the mystery plays and Coventry went the whole hog and performed on movable pageant wagons the Creation all the way through to Doomsday. The Coventry cycle was usually performed on the Feast of Corpus Christi, but later it was performed when needed.

The city trade guilds, along with the odd actor, produced the spectacle, starting at 5 am with the creation and Adam and Eve. Later came the birth of Christ accompanied by the Coventry Carol and the performance ended as night fell with the burning of a paper image of the world as Doomsday came. The plays were being performed as early as 1384 for in that year Richard II and his queen came to the city to see them. Others who saw them include Henry V, Henry VI, Henry VIII and Queen Elizabeth I. Another great who witnessed the event as a young man was William Shakespeare who later wrote in one of his plays, 'It out Herods Herod.' He was referring to the over-acting of Coventry's Herod who during the event ran amok amongst the crowd shouting and ranting like a mad man, waving a large sword above his head. Shakespeare also mentioned Coventry's notorious Devil who, much to the trepidation and amusement to the crowd, would leap from a flaming hell's mouth and drag an unsuspecting member of the audience kicking and screaming into hell.

Every year the Mystery Plays drew thousands to the city to view its spectacle but by 1584 England was becoming more puritanical and there were calls to see the plays ended. Coventry's traders didn't wish them to end as they brought great revenue to the city. A compromise was reached and a more politically correct Protestant play was produced called the *Destruction of Jerusalem*, but it was a flop as it held none of the wonder and colour of the original plays. Guilds tried to pull out and paid cash rather than take part in the play. In 1589 the city fathers allowed the original plays to be performed again but they were replaced again in 1591 with *Jerusalem*. The original mystery plays were not performed again until twenty-nine years ago when the Belgrade Theatre restarted the cycle, this time shorter and tailored to a modern audience, in the ruins of the old cathedral. The plays consist of the only two cycles to survive: the Shearman, Tailors and Weavers plays.

A Mystery Play pageant waggon by Spon Gate.

N

NEW HOUSE

New House is one of Coventry's older lost mansions, which stood on the corner of Keresley Road and Sadler Road. The superb domed and turreted Elizabethan gem was built as a country retreat outside the walls of Coventry. The site of New House was much older, previously housing a moated grange built by Coventry Priory and attached to a 436 acre fenced and ditched hunting park known as Whitmore Park. After the Dissolution the Grange came into the hands of Sir Ralph Sadler, who sold it on to John Hales of Whitefriars. On John Hales's death his property passed into the hands of his nephew, also known as John Hales. In the 1580s this John Hales decided to demolish the old monastic grange and build New House in the country with views of Coventry's three spires. He and his family moved into the completed property in 1586.

John Hales died in 1607, leaving a widow from his second marriage, three daughters and a son, once again called John. This third John Hales, like his father, married twice and in 1624 sold the New House to Sir Richard Burnaby for £1,138. Burnaby sold the property on to a gent called Cooke who in turn sold it to Sir Christopher Yelverton. The latter still owned the house in 1656, but within two years the property was rented by William Strode Esq. William, his wife and his four children all died during their occupancy, though history does not tell us why.

The next residents of the New House were the Bohun family. John Bohun

New House, Keresley, as it would have appeared in the late eighteenth century.

died in 1699 and a hugely expensive funeral was held for him at St Michael's church. His coffin was pulled by six black stallions, followed by twenty-five coaches, and his body was surrounded by 200 great candles in the church. His son George Bohun represented Coventry as its MP and resided in the house until his death. By 1721 the Bohun line ended with the death of Susanna Clarke (*nee* Bohun). Her husband continued to live in the house for a short time before moving on. Drawings based on the house in the Bohun's time show it to have been based around a central courtyard, with front, side and rear entrances. The building had around 150 windows, making it very light and airy inside. Outside the gardens were surrounded by a large wall and subdivided into seven walled gardens with classical statuary and geometrically laid out lawns and pathways. To the rear was a kitchen garden and above were orchards and an area called the 'Wilderness'.

After the Bohuns, the house had various occupants, the last being the Smiths before it was demolished in 1779. All that remained of this beautiful Elizabethan mansion were the balls and pillars at the Keresley Road entrance. These later led into the grounds of the Moat House, which grew larger and larger as the twentieth century approached, but it too suffered the same fate as the New House and was demolished in the 1920s as housing spread through the area.

NOD, MOUNT

Mount Nod is a prominence in the Eastern Green area of the city. Before being built over in the twentieth century the mount was the site of Mount Nod Farm. Under the farm a powerful spring pumped out huge quantities of water for centuries. The mount and its spring must have had ancient origins for 'Nod' comes from the Celtic god Nuada Argatlam or Nuada of the Silver Hand. Nuada was a nature god associated with the acts of hunting and healing. Nuada's healing power came through the waters that issued from the ground, thus springs became associated with the god and were sacred to him. In the Roman period the veneration of Nuada continued and the Romans called him Noden or Nod for short, hence Mount Nod.

O

OLD GRAMMAR SCHOOL (ST JOHN'S HOSPITAL)

What we now know as the old grammar school began life as part of a complex and church created in 1176 after Edmund, archdeacon of Coventry from 1160 to 1176, pleaded earnestly with Prior Laurence that better provision should be made for the aged and infirm travellers. The community was run

The Old Grammar School before the laying out of Hales Street.

by the knights hospitallers but continued under priory control and over the years was given endowments of land and buildings for its upkeep. The community consisted of brothers and sisters and in 1522 it held three priests, three clerks and five sisters and maintained thirty beds – within the house had forty poor and sometimes more. In Stowe's Annals it states that there were five priests and five sisters who continually kept ten beds for 'passengers and poor people' who might were allowed to stay for two nights and two days.

In the church the chancel and choir were reserved for religious purposes while the beds of the sick and infirm lined the nave and chancel walls. This part of the building still stands today, with its large decorated fourteenth-century window. John Blakemen and his wife gave one of the beds, on condition that 'no mad, quarrelsome, infected or loose person wandering the streets at night, was to be admitted to the bed'. The north transept remains but the south transept was pulled down in 1848 when Hales Street was built. Underneath the church are crypts and access still exists. Part of one goes underneath Hales Street towards the shops in the Burges. The Hospital of St John was dissolved by order of the crown and the building and land were soon after acquired by John Hales. He was involved, through the King's request, in founding a grammar school which shortly after its foundation moved into this building. Inside can still be found a number of medieval choir stalls which originated in Whitefriars church and were moved here when the building was converted into a grammar school. The stalls used as school desks and seats are covered with ancient graffiti, with games cut into the ancient oak by bored scholars.

A number of years ago an American offered to buy the building, have it taken down stone by stone and shipped to America. Canon Beaumont said at the time, 'If it is worth that to Americans, it is worth much more to the people of Coventry.' Sadly, over the years the building has suffered, as funds have been needed for essential work on Holy Trinity church and to date the building remains boarded up awaiting the restorer's hand.

OSBURGA

Very little can be said for certain about Coventry's St Osburga as her history, like that of many other Saxon saints, is fairly obscure. It is thought that Osburga, commonly referred to as Osburg, was one of the famed sisters of Barking mentioned as the 'Divine Fortress' by St Aldhelm, bishop of Sherborne. Aldhelm's book, *De laudibus virginitatis*, written around 675, says that Osburga and her sisters left the safety of Barking to set up other monastic houses around the country. Coventry's tradition of the saint, plus the existence of St Osburg's Pool and her relics, back the tradition that she set up a house in Coventry. Recent excavations of Coventry's later priory church suggest that Osburga's church was on the same site, Hill Top.

Only two written sources mention this house, a fourteenth-century manuscript in the Bodleian Library states: 'In ancient times on the banks of the river called by the inhabitants Sherbourne, which flows right through the city of Coventry, there was formerly a monastery of maidens dedicated to God.' John Rous, the fifteenth-century priest at Guy's Cliff, appears to have had access to many ancient documents. He wrote of Canute's harrying of Warwickshire in 1016, telling of the destruction of the Home Hill fortress at Stoneleigh, and he states: 'even the Abbey of Nuns at Coventry is destroyed, of which in times past the Virgin St Osburg was the Abbess'. The fact that he says 'is destroyed' and not 'was' suggests he is quoting from an original Saxon document.

After his devastation of the land Canute sought solace by restoring or rebuilding churches he had destroyed, especially those associated with local saints. This probably led to St Osburga's rebuilding and Canute's later reference to being the church's builder. A Saxon door jamb found in Palmer Lane in 1934 decorated with a squirrel in a tree probably belongs to the original church. During the excavation of the later priory a curved wall was discovered held together by green mortar. Curved asps and side aisles are common in seventh- and eighth-century Saxon churches and this was likely to be a surviving fragment of Osburga's later restored and possibly extended church. Below this curved wall lay an eighth-century burial, probably in situ in the graveyard of the original church. The surviving main relic of St Osburga, namely her head, survived into the later monastery church then cathedral of St Mary. In 1462 her remains were translated into a new shrine within the cathedral.

In 1868 while workmen were clearing rubble and soil for the building of Blue Coat school a seal was found, with a figure cut into it showing Osburga standing with a crozier in her left hand and her name cut around the outer edge. In 1302 the Warwickshire Crown Pleas state

Saxon door jamb.

that the Feast of St Osburga was on 23 January. In 1410 John Burghill, bishop of Coventry and Lichfield, ordered St Osburga's Day be kept.

☛ *See* PILGRIMS

P

PALACE YARD

Palace Yard which stood in Earl Street was believed to have been built in the sixteenth century by the Hopkins family who resided here until 1822. One of the most notable occupants of the house was Richard Hopkins, sheriff of Coventry, who appears to have been a grocer by trade. Richard had much sympathy for the martyr Robert Glover and wanted to release him. His compassion was also shown to another religious prisoner to whom he lent an unauthorized religious book. For this in 1555 he was arrested and imprisoned. John Bradford the martyr wrote:

> *To the end of the world it shall be written for a memorial to you praise that Richard Hopkins, sheriff of Coventry, for conscience to do his office before God, was cast into the Fleet, and there kept prisoner for a long time . . . Who would have thought that you should be the first magistrate, that for Christ's sake should have lost anything.*

Hopkins didn't suffer any further for he had many powerful friends who eventually obtained his release. Thereafter with his wife and eight children he left England and spent the rest of Bloody Mary's reign in exile in Basle, returning only after her death.

In the past there has often been confusion between which Elizabeth stayed at the Palace Yard. It is definite that the Princess Elizabeth stayed here. It is however interesting that I have found references to Queen Elizabeth I coming to Coventry on more than one visit, apart from the 1565 visit. It appears that the historian Fretton recorded in the Birmingham and Midland Archaeological Society's journal of 1872, from documents burned in the Birmingham Library fire, that Queen Elizabeth stayed at Palace Yard on a second visit in 1587, when she was again expected at Whitefriars. This has yet to be proven but is still worth recording.

On 5 November 1605 Princess Elizabeth, daughter of James I, was brought here for protection against the Gunpowder Plotters. In 1687 James II stayed here and was said to have celebrated mass and feasted with many other nobles in the banqueting room over the arch of the second courtyard. The following year Princess Anne of Denmark stayed here. Edward Hopkins afterwards wrote of the event:

At the latter end of the year 1688 the Prince of Orange landing in the West, and Prince George of Denmark going to him, his Princess, Anne, the King's youngest daughter was put under confinement at St James's . . . she made her escape in the middle of the night . . . She made long journeys till she reached Nottingham and from thence came to Coventry to my father's house, where during her sojourn, part of three days, she received an account by express that the King, who

Palace Yard around 1902.

was before fled . . . to London, had abandoned that city upon the Prince of Orange marching towards it . . . Upon this the Princess Anne sat forth for London.

Hopkins says that on that very night a rumour had spread throughout the city that the King's Irish papist army were 'destroying all by fire and sword'. He adds: 'It was no wonder I had the most dreadful apprehensions and it was by the whole family increased from my father's being absent, for he had gone to escort the Princess, a day or two on her journey to London.' In 1690 the Hopkins household had its last royal visitor, Anne's brother, Prince George of Denmark.

When the last of the Hopkins family left in 1822 the building was sold. At this time Coventry historian William Reader purchased the two Alexander the Great tapestries from the tapestry room which lay next to the state or banqueting room; these can still be seen in the upper lobby of St Mary's Hall. The building was then converted to a coaching inn called the Golden Horse and for many years an old painted sign still survived giving the time of the coaches. On 9 December 1831 the Golden Horse was put up for auction at the Craven Arms. It was described thus:

Lot 1. All that capital and Roomy INN called or known by the sign of the Old Golden Horse Tavern, situate in Earl Street, with stables, brew house, and other premises, now occupied by Mr John Lloyd, together with two Pieces of Land fronting to Earl Street suitable for the erection of two Retail Shops and ample yard room, behind having a long frontage to a proposed thoroughfare, to be called the Old Palace Court.

Lot 2 consisted of the rest of the building, which included the banqueting or state room over the inner second gateway: 'The ancient Palace and State Rooms of Queen Elizabeth with Land adjoining for the protection of the present Lights, or for the expansion of the Buildings, subject to the thoroughfare called the Old Palace Court.' (The thoroughfare was in fact a pathway which led through Palace Yard and took a westerly direction through and out of Little Palace Yard in Little Park Street.)

Lot 3 was simply described as 'The Roomy Dwelling House occupied by Mr John Smith, in front of the Palace Court and on the opposite side of it to Lot 1.' This was later to become the offices of the *Coventry Herald*.

It is clear from the auctioneer's catalogue that, rightly or wrongly, they or the previous owner believed Queen Elizabeth stayed here. It was through the previous owner that the lawned area at the rear acquired the name 'Palace Lawn', which no doubt led to the creation of the name for the thoroughfare, 'The Old Palace Court'.

In the late nineteenth century it was acquired by builder J. Ackroyd who used it as a builder's yard. It was still known then as the Golden Horse Yard and it was Ackroyd himself who renamed it Palace Yard and had a painted sign bearing the name fitted onto the outside of the building. Before the First World War Palace Yard was converted into craft shops, including the premises of Winifred King who specialized in making beautiful objects in silver. Palace Yard was destroyed by a single large high-explosive bomb on the night of 14 November 1940.

PARKES, HENRY

Henry Parkes was born in 1815 at Moat House Cottage in Moat House Lane, Canley. He was the youngest son of a tenant farmer and as Canley was then on the Stoneleigh Estate he was baptized at Stoneleigh church and attended school in that village. Later the family fell on hard times and moved to Birmingham and Henry was apprenticed to an ivory turner. Henry quickly prospered in his trade and began to take an active interest in debates and politics. In 1836 he married Clarinda Varney from Kenilworth and the couple moved to London seeking a better life.

All initially went well and their first children were born, but times changed and the business failed. Worse still, Henry and Clarinda's children died and this was what drove them to leave England in the hope of a better life in Australia. They set up a fancy goods shop in Sydney selling, amongst other things, Henry's delicate turned work. Once the business prospered Henry again began to take an interest in politics and joined a movement whose aims were to end the transportation of convicts to the colony. By 1850 he had become leader of the movement and had started a political newspaper called *The Empire* with which he fought the many injustices he found in his new home.

In May 1854 at the age of 39 he was elected as representative of Sydney to the New South Wales parliament and he fought for the improvement of life for the colony's small farmers. He also fought for better hospitals and prisons and brought together the six Australian colonies into one state. His popularity soared and in 1878 he was made the first Prime Minister of New South Wales, an office which he held five times. In 1882 he was knighted by Queen Victoria and became Sir Henry Parkes. He died on 30 April 1896 and his standing is reflected in the fact that 30,000 mourners attended his funeral. His cottage still stands, tucked away behind Canley Fire Station, and continues to be a place of pilgrimage to Australians who call him 'The Father of the Federation'. In 2001 the face of the Coventry-born son of a farmer replaced the head of the Queen on the Australian five dollar banknote.

PARKES, JOHN

At the side of St Michael's Avenue near the old cathedral lies the grave of John Parkes, a Coventry worthy who for many years caused great speculation as to his trade. His gravestone, which is in fact the second stone used, bears this inscription:

> *To the memory of John Parkes, a Native of this City.*
> *He was a man of Mild Disposition, a Gladiator by*
> *Profession, who, after having fought 350 battles in*
> *the principal parts of Europe, with honour and applause,*
> *at length quitted the stage, sheathed his sword, and*
> *with Christian Resignation submitted to the Great*
> *Victor, in the 52nd year of his age, anno 1733.*

Some have suggested Parkes was a prize fighter, or fencing master, or even a preacher. John Parkes was exactly was his stone states: a gladiator. He was an expert at fighting with a 3¹/₂ foot razor-tipped sword on a raised circular stage. His second weapon of choice was the flail. Parkes was known throughout Europe as one of the finest gladiators who fought for money – not until death but until one opponent refused or was unable to carry on. It was a bloody affair and a common thing for such fighters to be extremely scarred as open wounds were often stitched up while they drank a glass of claret between rounds.

Parkes, being an expert at the art, was less scarred than others, his technique was described as slow, methodical and precise. It was said that his precision with the sword was so great that he could catch coins thrown at him on the tip of the blade. A surviving document for a combat at the Bear Garden in London in 1710 has the formidable Parkes issuing a challenge to Thomas Hesgate for several combats with the back sword, sword and buckler, sword and dagger, the falchion and the quarterstaff.

Not surprisingly Parke's reputation spread far and wide and those who fought him boasted of doing so. Timothy Buck of London, 'master of the science', on accepting a challenge from another gladiator replies through the press, 'I, Timothy Buck . . . hearing Miller did fight Mr Parkes of Coventry, will not fail (God willing) to meet this fair inviter'. John Parkes, known as Parkes the Invincible, became a national sporting hero, like his friend James Fig, of fencing and boxing fame. The nation mourned his death in 1733, and thereafter John's brother Thomas carried on the art, but never attained the fame of his brother.

PEEPING TOM

Peeping Tom, the man who looked out on Godiva and was struck blind, is known throughout the world, despite the fact that he never existed. His link to the ride is much later and comes from a classical story of the voyeur who peeps at the naked goddess and is struck blind. The figure of Tom in his window wasn't recorded until the seventeenth century when a certain John Warren wrote, 'Beeing in Couentry in the yer 1659, and at the end of the stret going to the Cross, out of the window stands a statu of a man. I asked on of the cittezens what it ment [and he] related this story [of Godiva].' It has been generally assumed that Peeping Tom appeared around the time of the first recorded procession in 1678, but this shows the image was in use during the dying days of the more austere Commonwealth. The oak figure used to represent Tom appears to be a fifteenth-century statue of St George, probably originating in the priory or St George's chapel. The statue had its arms removed so it could be fitted against various windows. The back of the statue also has a large section gouged out of it by various tourists taking the wood as a memento. At the time of the Godiva processions the figure would always disappear from its nook and reappear dressed in a fancy cockaded hat and sometimes newly painted.

An 1860s engraving of the Peeping Tom statue, based on a photograph by Wingrave.

In 1678 the figure was moved from near the Cross to a nook at the bottom of Greyfriars Lane. When that house was pulled down in 1775, Thomas Sharp acquired the figure and had it placed in a special window in his shop in Smithford Street. When Hertford Street was opened in 1813 Sharp's shop became the corner building and Tom was placed in a corner nook so he looked across the new street towards Broadgate. In the late 1870s the King's Head was rebuilt on a larger scale, taking in the site of Sharp's shop, and the figure of Tom found himself in the corner nook of a new grander building. Here he stayed until about 1936 when he was removed to the lounge of the newly refurbished hotel and his image was replaced in the window with a plaster copy. In November 1940 the King's Head was destroyed but Tom was saved and placed for safety in the vaults of Lloyds Bank. In March 1991 Tom found a new home in Cathedral Lanes looking out over the Godiva statue.

PHILLIPS, JOHN

John Phillips lived during the eighteenth century and is certainly not a man of merit; Phillips was a noted notorious criminal who history would have forgotten had someone not written a pamphlet on his life in 1790. Phillips was born in Wales in 1761, the son of a farmer of good repute. His dislike for education brought him early into the family business, but like many a farmer's boy he yearned for adventure and at the age of 19 he joined the crew of an armed privateer. During this expedition Phillips was captured by the French and imprisoned for over a year. He was then ordered to be transported but the ship he was on struck a rock and sank. Phillips was rescued by smugglers and within weeks became a crew member of another privateer destined for Lisbon.

In Lisbon Phillips and a fellow crew man were trusted with £30 to acquire more crew but they chose to flee with the money. The money spent, Phillips joined a frigate which while at sea captured two privateers then sailed for England. Back in England he joined the fleet and sailed under Admiral Hood to Barbados. Here Phillips with a new partner in crime robbed two officers and escaped across the island on a stolen mule before boarding the *Nancy* and sailing back to England. A year later Phillips seemed to have settled and worked as a servant in Shropshire. His master however turned out to be a villain himself and was forced to flee the country.

Phillips then moved in with a miller's wife but the business under his management suffered and the mill was seized and sold. Undaunted and armed with a brace of pistols Phillips managed to steal the £300 the mill had raised and rode off for Liverpool. Three weeks later he was incarcerated in Shrewsbury Gaol but had to be released as he could not be positively identified. Phillips then left with the miller's wife back to Liverpool and continued his career of defrauding people and highway robbery. He moved to London and set up as a cheese factor, giving a respectable face to his criminal background.

He joined a gang and with them began robbing stage coaches and anything on the road travelling through London, Bristol, Bath and Oxford. Phillips was arrested in London and condemned to death, but two days before he was to hang the sentence was changed to transportation, thanks to the intervention of his uncle who was a farrier to the King. Phillips was placed on board a transport ship but escaped before it set sail and he rode off for Ireland on his favourite horse. However, he changed course and went back to London and the gang and the robberies.

After three years he moved to Bath and married a young woman from a respectable family, took the dowry of £40 and rode off into the sunset and while on that road to Maidenhead managed to relieve an Irish gent of £200.

Phillips continued his criminal career and eventually moved into the Warwickshire area where he hired a chaise from Mr Townsend of Warwick. Townsend suspected fraud and Phillips was arrested and placed in Warwick Gaol. On his release he became associated with Matthew Archer of Birmingham. Phillips told Archer that while he was in gaol he was told that there was a club that met at the Shepherd and Shepherdess in Keresley, Coventry. The men decided to take the first opportunity to rob it.

The men rode to Coventry and stopped at the Nag's Head, near the canal basin, then walked to Keresley to the Shepherd, but decided to hold back, Phillips returned to the Nag and Archer to Birmingham. Here Archer met Anthony Farnsworth, a sawyer, who returned with him to Coventry seeking work. They met up with Phillips and Farnsworth was reluctantly talked into taking part in the robbery. The men walked to the Shepherd and Shepherdess and armed with pistols terrorized the old man who ran it and his niece. They left with £10, some clothes and some other items. The men then strolled back across the fields of Radford to the Radford Bowling Green and there rested. Phillips was later jolted from his sleep by armed men sent by Alderman Hewitt. Archer and Farnsworth had disappeared with the cash and goods.

Phillips wasted no time in naming his accomplices and within days the others were taken. Phillips, manacled in Coventry Gaol, told his tale, and then on 18 August 1790, Phillips, Archer and Farnsworth were hanged before a huge crowd on Whitley Common. It is reported that on the gallows he 'called to the executioner to make haste . . . and he would have leapt off the cart . . . had not pains been taken to prevent him'. The pamphlet of Phillips's life ends with these words, 'Thus lived and died one of the most accomplished villains that ever disgraced human nature.'

PILGRIMS

Ancient Coventry always attracted a number of pilgrims coming to visit its cathedral church and pray to some of its holy relics. The earliest recorded major relic in Coventry was the remains, later just the head, of St Osburga, the founding abbess of Coventry's seventh- to eighth-century nunnery. This was first kept in St Osburga's and later translated to the late Saxon church. The first major relic to be added to Osburg's was the arm of St Augustine of Hippo. Canute ordered Archbishop Aethelnoth to purchase the arm in Pavia for 100 talents of silver and one talent of gold. The great relic was presented to the church of Coventry in 1022 and placed upon the relic beam.

Over time the earlier church was gradually swallowed up within the great priory church and more relics were added. To cope with the growing numbers of pilgrims the church built a guest house in Palmer Lane to house its visitors and take their cash. Badges of these pilgrims covering many shrines, such as

Walsingham and St James in Spain, were dredged out of the Sherbourne in Palmer Lane in the nineteenth century.

In 1539 the Dissolution of the Monasteries meant that such relics were listed. At Coventry, they were: a copper shrine of St Osburga, St Osburga's head enclosed in a gilded case, a piece of the holy cross mounted in silver and gilt, a relic of Thomas à Becket, a piece of the Virgin Mary's tomb, a bone from St Cecily's foot, a bone of St James mounted in a jewelled silver and gilt cross, an image of St George with a bone encased in silver or mounted on a silver shield, the arms of St Augustine, Jerome, Justin and Sibvine encased in silver and gilt, a relic of St Andrew, a rib of St Laurence, a relic of St Catherine. Also an image of one of the children of Israel and a shrine to the apostles, a barrel of relics of confessors, four 'little' crosses, two bags of assorted relics and a phial of Our Lady's milk.

Those who prayed to these relics could also visit the nationally known statue in a painted room in a tower by London Road Gate. The figure inside and a painting of it on the outside was known as 'Our Lady of the Tower' and was believed to protect those on the road to London. Those who did not visit the image would salute the painting of it as they passed; this practice gave a name to a nearby inn, the Salutation. John Blomstone, examined for heresy in 1485, mentions the tower, saying: 'It is foolishness to go on a pilgrimage to the image of Our Lady of Doncaster, Walsingham, or of the Tower of Coventry, for a man might as well worship the Blessed Virgin by the fireside in the kitchen . . .'
☞ *See* **OSBURGA, COVENTRY PRIORY**

POLICE
Since Coventry received its governing charter in 1345 it has had a form of policing in the city maintained by the City Leet. The latter also created the various by-laws in the Old Council Chamber in St Mary's Hall, crying out all the new laws from a balcony, the blocked-in doorway of which can still be seen on the front of the building. Throughout the ages reputable individuals were given the status of watchman and would patrol the city streets dealing with any breach of the common law. The Easter Leet of 1450 records: 'Ordained that 40 decent men of good and honest behaviour and bodily strength shall keep watch from 9 pm to the ringing of the day bell. Which men shall be dressed in jacks, sallets, poleaxes or glaves.'

From the late seventeenth century the watchmen met at the Watch House in the Market Square at 10 o'clock at night. They would then go on their rounds and return to warm themselves then go around again and that's how it was all night. Watch boxes like sentry boxes were placed at various points, such as Cross Cheaping, the bottom of Hertford Street and the bottom of

A fine-looking group of Coventry policemen in 1945.

Gosford Street. There were other resting places too, such as a recessed doorway in the east wall of St John's in Hill Street that was used by up to three watchmen.

In the eighteenth century magistrates such as three-times mayor of Coventry John Hewitt took their role very seriously indeed and made a career out of thief-taking. Indeed Hewitt spent a good part of his own income on keeping the streets of Coventry safe. Hewitt was based in the Mayor's Parlour, which was effectively the centre of justice and policing in the city on the boundary of Broadgate and Cross Cheaping. The building was first acquired in 1573 and received considerable alterations and extensions in the 1770s. During this period Criminal Associations were also founded such as the 'Comb, Binley, Wyken, Sow and Calledon Association' which met at the Craven Arms, Binley, and offered rewards for the capture of felons.

In 1835 the Municipal Corporation Act made it a requirement that every borough in the land should form and maintain its own police force. Coventry already had a force of a kind led by Thomas Henry Prosser, an ex-Bow Street Runner who took the position of chief constable in 1832. Prosser however was the sole paid member of the force, something which the new Act deemed inadequate, and on 7 March 1836 Prosser led the newly formed paid

Coventry force which consisted of himself, an inspector, sergeant and twenty constables. One of these constables was Samuel Deeming, who in September 1845 arrested one of his regulars George Chittem. Brought up before the justices Chittem was described as 'a most incorrigible drunkard . . . in a wretched and filthy condition, charged with being drunk and incapable of looking after himself. He said it was some time before he had been brought before the court and if the magistrates would but excuse him this once, he would endeavour to keep sober.' He was allowed one more chance to reform, and discharged. Sadly for him Chittem didn't manage to reform and spent most of his waking life in the stocks.

Prosser ran a tight ship for many years and during his time justice and police business left the Mayor's Parlour, which was sold, and was transferred to St Mary's Hall, when the Old Mayoress's Parlour became the Justice Room. Prosser retired in 1857 and Thomas Skermer of the Liverpool Police took over his role. Skermer stayed until 1861, making a sudden disappearance when the Watch Committee began investigating the accounts. Skermer's sudden disappearance brought Prosser out of retirement until Chief Constable John Norris could be appointed in 1862, the year before the service transferred to St Mary's Street.

Norris stayed twenty-eight years and was replaced in 1890 by Alexander Gray, who in turn was replaced in 1899 by Charles Charsley. In 1969 the Coventry force was amalgamated with the county force and became the Warwickshire and Coventry Constabulary. Further changes quickly followed in 1974 when political boundary changes forced the Coventry and Solihull forces to be transferred to the West Midlands Police Force and so it has remained ever since.

☛ *See* STOCKS

POOL MEADOW

Pool Meadow began life as part of the Bablake which stretched through the low ground between Broadgate and Barrs Hill. In a much shrunken form it is later associated with the Priory Mill which stood before and after the existence of Coventry Priory. It is said that when the mill ceased to function the remaining pool began to silt up and eventually became little more than marshland. The land was owned by the Bablake Boy's Charity and in the 1850s the marshland was drained and quickly became usable. The corporation paid the charity £30 a year for the meadow and raised £130 a year from 1859 to 1888 when Coventry's yearly Great Fair was held there. In 1888 the corporation paid £3,000 for the meadow and the following year purchased other adjoining land towards Cox Street.

For most of its later history the meadow was an open space used mainly as

The Great Fair being held on Pool Meadow in 1920. The decorated building in the background is the Coventry Baths.

a bus station. In the nineteenth and early twentieth century it was often associated with major school rallies and events such as the Godiva procession when it would be used as a starting point. The site is now half bus station and half car park, with a bingo hall thrown in.

PRECINCT

In 1938 Coventry City Council employed its first city architect Donald Gibson. It was their intention over time to knock down streets such as Smithford Street and to modernize and widen them. Other ideas put forward suggest the redevelopment of Broadgate. Gibson's role had previously been part of the job of Ernest Ford the city engineer. It was Ford who originally put forward the idea of a traffic-free precinct. After Gibson's appointment Ford could get little backing for his ideas. Gibson, however, quickly built up an office of young architects and soon put forward a proposal to redevelop a large part of the central area including Broadgate and the Cathedral Quarter,

The Upper Precinct in the early 1960s.

where he envisaged offices, museums, libraries and civic buildings. But before the bulldozers moved in the Luftwaffe struck, leaving an open canvas for rebuilding. In February 1941 Gibson and Ford both put forward plans for the rebuilding and Gibson's was accepted. It consisted of a single-level development running down from Broadgate, with a central water feature. By 1945 the water feature was confined to the upper part and a road was added running through it. Work began with the ceremonial laying of the Phoenix Stone in the Upper Precinct. Work then started on Broadgate Island to which the Godiva statue was added in 1949. The first building erected in Broadgate was Broadgate House, followed by the Hotel Leofric and the Upper Precinct, a revised design which Gibson based on the Rows at Chester.

The Upper Precinct was completed in 1955. Work then began on Market Way, with its road, just before Gibson left in January 1955. He was replaced by Arthur Ling who began by stopping the proposed road. He redesigned the Lower Precinct as it was shown that people did not use the upper level of the Upper Precinct. Ling also decided that the development needed more height and added tower blocks such as Mercia House. He also built the Locarno to bring some nightlife into an area of pure business. Ling also designed the

Belgrade Theatre, opened in 1958, and the Herbert Art Gallery and Museum in 1960, both presently undergoing reconstruction.

PREHISTORY

Coventry has a lot of potential as a prehistoric site. There is the huge prehistoric landscape on the site of Warwick University with houses, enclosures, domestic, ritual and burial mounds. This area also brought to light three stone axe heads carried from Craig Llwyd in Caernarvonshire. In the early twentieth century a stone battle axe was found during building work in Green Lane and in 1968, in a garden in Greendale Road, a perforated comptonite stone axe head was found. Less than one and a half miles away an axe hammer of the same period was found by Pickford Brook.

In the 1920s a crude pot was found at King's Hill, Finham, dating back to 1500 BC. A Bronze Age axe was discovered on the old Whitley Aerodrome site at a depth of 3 feet, resting on sandstone. Significantly, there was once thought to be a prehistoric hill fort on Whitley Common and an ancient hollow way which led from it was luckily recorded before its destruction by unemployed weavers in the 1860s when the common was flattened.

Other items have been found nearer the city centre. In 1947, when workmen were excavating Broadgate within 15 feet of the present Godiva statue, they found a Bronze Age axe head dating to around 650 BC. Later, amongst the spoil from these excavations, a second axe head was found. The first axe head was forgotten and the second dismissed in the 1960s as an archaeologist believed that the axe head may have come from Shelton's Museum which he thought was blown up in Broadgate. In reality Shelton's Museum wasn't blown up, nor was it in Broadgate, so the axe, like the previous one, was an actual Broadgate find. The significance of this is even greater as there are two of them. One could be a casual loss but two on a hill top could relate to a deliberate ritual burial, as an offering to the sky gods. This isn't the only ancient axe head to be found in the centre of Coventry, as an obscure reference from the Staunton Collection tells of one ancient palstave being found in the city centre on or near the site of one of the Pageant Houses. In St Mary's Hall was once kept an ancient spoon called the 'Lady's Spoon' which was said to be an ancient scapula.

Near Broadgate other items have been discovered, such as a log boat and coracle paddle. Interestingly, when Market Way was being constructed in the late 1940s, workmen unearthed hundreds of oak piles sticking out of the ancient lake bed. This area was not settled in the medieval period so the oak piles may have dated from an earlier time. Oak piles sticking out of lake beds are more commonly associated with prehistoric crannogs or lake villages. Nearby in 1935–6 on the site of British Home Stores on the old lake shore rough black pottery was found; this could have been prehistoric or possibly later Saxon.

Up until the early twentieth century a large mound stood in Primrose Hill Park, known locally as the Giant's Grave. The mound, like all other 'Giant's Graves', appears to have been a prehistoric burial mound, planted on a hill top. Sometime in the early twentieth century, the mound was flattened, only to be replaced later with a second mound of spoil which was later excavated mistakenly for the original. There was once a large mound in the churchyard of St Michael used as a moot or meeting mound. It is quite common for moot mounds to have begun life as prehistoric burial mounds and so this may have been. Significantly churches dedicated to St Michael are commonly found on high pagan prehistoric sites.

Possible prehistoric sites are scattered across the city. One which is possibly a ritual site lies in the playing fields of what was Copthorne School in Keresley. Here from the air, when conditions are right, can be seen a large circular ditched enclosure, possibly a henge ritual site surrounded by a ditch about 15 feet across. Track ways can also be seen leading into the ditched enclosure and a short distance away to the north-west can be seen a line of ritual pits. Another prehistoric enclosure can be found a short distance away along a lane which joins Keresley to Allesley. This ancient lane follows a fairly straight line until it reaches the enclosure then curves around it. Significantly in this area was recently found a harness fitting from a Celtic chariot, showing that people of significance and wealth crossed this area in the Bronze and Iron Age. This was confirmed some years ago by the finding of a Gallo-Belgic gold stater dating from 57–45 BC in a garden in Beake Avenue.

Coombe Abbey, from the Celtic 'cwn', once had a number of round barrows in its grounds and also a large standing stone. There are other possible round barrow sites leading off into Coombe Fields and heading towards the great tumuli which later formed Brinklow Castle. Another standing stone known locally as the 'Donkey Stone' stood until the nineteenth century near the corner of Foleshill and Old Church Road. A name associated with the Earlsdon and Hearsall district is Whorwell or Horwell. This refers to a depopulated hamlet and a lane called Whor Lane. The word 'Whor' is significant as it probably refers to Whor or Hoar stones, usually standing stones associated with prehistoric sites. The positioning of large stones by wells or springs is also very significant and was probably the origin of Whorwell itself. Such stones and wells could also once be found in Radford and at King's Hill at Finham.

☛ *See* **IRON AGE VILLAGE**

PRIZE FIGHTING

Prize fighting in Coventry was a popular sport. It had been popularized by fencing master James Fig, starting in London and spreading to the provinces. One place for prize fights in Coventry was on Whitley Common near the gallows which stood in the far corner of the common by Howes Lane. In April 1829 local fighters fought a 'pitched battle' on Whitley Common: Bill Hayfield the 'Flash Barber' and Bob Smith. Hayfield won after one hour and received the purse of £2 a side. Unusually a second fight followed between the butcher, Bacon Smith, and Peter Smith. The *Herald* reported that, 'This battle lasted about 28 minutes, during which seven such desperate rounds were fought, as are seldom witnessed by the admirers of the science. Bacon proved the victor.' In July the 'Flash Barber' fought and defeated Jack Hammerton the 'Chicken Butcher' behind Hammerton's Mill in the city centre.

In November 1850 one of Coventry's more notable fighters John 'Jack' 'Fatty' Adrian fought Nuneaton fighter Bill Betteridge for 40 sovereigns in a field near the Engine public house in Longford. Betteridge, the stronger of the two men, had a lame arm which he called his 'vice'. The vice was used to lock on to his opponent's head while the other administered the blows. Adrian and Betteridge fought 103 rounds over 2½ hours before the local 'beaks' intervened and brought the match to an end. Adrian had taken a beating but it was recorded that Betteridge looked as fresh as he was at the beginning. The two men later fought again and Adrian got the upper hand.

The following year Coventry fighters Ginger Berry and Harry Hodson from Longford fought on Whitley Common for 5 sovereigns a side. This was probably the quickest fight locally and was reported thus: 'In the first round Ginger hit his opponent under the right ear which laid him prostrate on the ground, and his seconds were unable to bring him to the scratch on time and Ginger was declared the victor, without having received a single blow.'

At this time prize fighting was actually illegal and was often stopped by local magistrates who sent constables to intervene. Despite this, in December 1836 local pugilists 'Game one Shilton' and 'Whopper Flint' met for £10 a side. A huge crowd followed them from Coventry where the magistrates had forbidden the fight and headed south. Warwickshire constables kept them moving, but by 'stealth' the crowd unexpectedly headed back for Coventry and set up a roped ring by Whitley Gallows and the two men fought there for an hour, with the match finally going to Shilton. Magistrates had failed to stop it and despite its illegality it was, like all such fights, covered in the *Coventry Herald* under 'Sporting Intelligence'. Prize fighting was very popular and drew thousands, from the poor to the rich, thus no doubt magistrates didn't always try too hard to stop more notable fights.

Two prize fighters battling it out.

Many fighters came from the butchery trade and many with their winnings bought their own public houses home to the 'fancy' as the sports followers were called. The main Coventry prize fighters' pubs where the fancy met and sparring took place were the Royal Oak, Hand in Heart and Golden Cup in Gosford Street, also the Stag in Bishop Street and the Sword and Mace in Earl Street. The two last inns were known throughout the world of prize fighting and were run by famed prize ring trainer William King.

The *Coventry Herald* of 27 July 1829 lists a number of local fighters who sparred at the Royal Oak, on one evening these were James Reading, known as the 'Living Skeleton', Ginger Berry, Bacon Smith, Fatty Adrian, Slogger Russell, Buck Gutteridge, Lun Caldicot, Long Waist Gilbert, Traveller Walker, Trainer Walker, Young Tip, Out and Out Ostler and the Pride of the Wharf. With the later introduction of Queensbury Rules the prize fight would go mainstream and was no longer illegal.

☛ *See* **PADDY GILL**

Q

QUADRANT
The area now known as the Quadrant was originally open land outside the city wall. In the seventeenth century temporary houses were built here to escape the plague which raged in the city. The area itself was later known as the 'Sheriff's Orchard' and was basically an enclosed apple orchard. The

buildings known as the Quadrant were built in the early to mid-nineteenth century and provided homes to some notable citizens, including the writer Angela Brazil.

R

RADFORD BOULDER

In a field behind Warden's farm in the village of Radford was once a spring-fed ancient well, known by locals as the Saxon Well. In the seventeenth century the King family used water from this well to supply their brewery in Well Street and it is believed that one of that family was responsible for placing the large syenite granite boulder on top of the well and had his initials AK cut into the well. The boulder, said to be of a type which was not found in England, was thought to have been carried to Radford by a glacier. The fact that it probably anciently stood near this well and the springs may have some ancient significance. After the last of the Warden family died the farm was sold for house building and in October 1913 the famed Radford Boulder was blown up with dynamite. Local historians were outraged and the notable historian 'Spectator' visited the site for the *Coventry Herald*. He wrote:

> *I climbed over the iron hurdles and plodded over the wet land, and there was the old well uncovered. The sandstone kerb was nearly all in position, but the boulder was gone. A great fragment of it lay close by, with an iron stanchion attached .. . the well seemed just an ordinary well, probably three feet in diameter, with the water rising to within three feet from the top, and round it, as I have said was the sandstone kerb on which the stone had rested.*

Spectator continued: 'This great stone, to which an end has now been put, had been a constant source of curiosity for generation after generation . . . quite a number of stories, one of which was that it marked the centre of England . . . many people have been found who believe this tradition to be true.' The surviving fragments of the boulder were gathered and cemented back together and the restored boulder was placed in Radford churchyard. Unbelievably in November 1940 Radford church was completely destroyed by a single landmine. With the church went a number of gravestones and the famed Radford Boulder. One fragment now survives in a bungalow wall in Corley.

RADFORD WAR MEMORIAL

The memorial was the first to be officially unveiled in the city after the Great War. It stands 8 foot 6 inches high and bears bronze panels with the names of 152 Radford men who went to war, seventeen of whom died and are highlighted by crosses. The memorial was unveiled on Radford Common by Councillor C Vernon Pugh on 20 December 1919 and dedicated by Yeatman-Biggs, bishop of Coventry. Vernon Pugh, manager of Rudge Cycles who lived at Radford House, paid for the memorial after the idea was brought to his attention by a village committee. The memorial was moved in the 1980s from the common across the road to a grass area by the rebuilt St Nicholas church. Sadly this first city memorial in recent years has suffered repeated vandalism.

ROMAN REMAINS

For most of its modern history the possibility that Coventry had any Roman history was generally dismissed. The *Victoria County History of Warwickshire* reinforces this belief and even dismisses a coin of Nero found in Broadgate in the eighteenth century. However, a number of Roman finds have been made in Coventry over the centuries. The first recorded Roman find in the area was quite large. In December 1792 labourers at Bullester Fields Farm in Foleshill were digging a trench, when at about 2 feet below the surface one struck an earthen pot which on examination was found to contain 1,800 coins from the reigns of Constantine, Constans, Constantius and Magentius. When the men returned to work on the trench in early January 1793 another pot was found packed with more coins. It was reported in the *Gentlemen's Magazine*: 'a second pot was much broken when discovered, but appears from the fragments to resemble the former, only is smaller; the coins though said to be better preserved, and larger are precisely the same sorts . . . as those first discovered'.

The placing of this hoard supports the likelihood that an ancient track way used by the Romans passed through Coventry. One probable route follows the Foleshill and Longford Road – Longford is a name often associated with Roman roads. The Leet Book says, in 1423: 'from the hye way that is callyd Sewall Pavement, pe [the] whiche leedyth from Coventre to Leycestre'. The idea of a paved road running from Coventry to Leicester in 1423 is impossible unless of course it was a Roman road, not actually paved in the modern sense but made up of stone with ditches either side. The actual route of the Sewell Pavement was the Stoney Stanton Road and this road does actually follow a line to Leicester if we assume some of the road has disappeared under the fields.

The ancient track way appears to enter Coventry via Barrs Hill, an area which has a legendary attachment to Agricola, who is said to have built a camp here and named the nearby settlement 'Coventina', after the Romano/Celtic water goddess. This isn't simply legend for in the past Roman

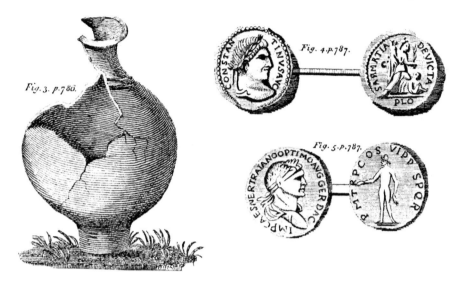

Part of the Foleshill hoard, showing coins of Constantinus and Trajanus.

pottery and coins have been discovered on Barrs Hill, mirroring the periods occupied by the Lunt Fort at Baginton. Also, in the nineteenth century, a 'medal' bearing the image of Coventina was found in the city centre.

The suggested track way would follow the line of Bishop/Silver Street and would have at one point crossed the lake between Barrs Hill and Broadgate Hill. When J B Shelton excavated at the bottom of Bishop Street he discovered by the lakeside Roman horse shoes known as hippo sandals and a Roman quern. He revealed a wooden causeway crossing the lake which he stated was Roman. In 1796, at a 'considerable' depth, an alabaster statuette of a laurel-crowned warrior was unearthed here. This was near a place mentioned in a fourteenth-century charter as having ruined remains of an ancient pillared building. The tradition of an ancient structure here was well known to the priests of St John's Hospital even in the sixteenth century. As late as 1868 it was noted: 'Under the Free Grammar School and round about it precincts are occasionally to be found masses of foundation walls and pillars of great strength and size.' One large round column base survived at the rear of the grammar school for many years.

In 1868 it was written that: 'A little south of the site [below Broadgate] of houses pulled down in 1820 are foundations of groined cellars and still deeper traces of an old pavement, said to be Roman, discovered during the excavations of a sewer some years ago.' Across from where Shelton discovered the causeway in the 1930s a small marble statue of the Roman god Mars was discovered and over the years pieces of an ancient track way associated with finds of Roman coins have been found going up Broadgate Hill, cutting through the area we now know as Broadgate. Broadgate itself has turned up Roman coins in the past, as have many other parts of central Coventry and the suburbs, such as Radford, Coundon, Stoke, Longford, Walsgrave, Hearsall and Willenhall, which was once the home to a Roman farm or villa.

The most recent Roman discovery was in the very heart of the city. In 2006 archaeologists from Birmingham University were excavating an area next to the entrance to Coventry University in Priory Street when they unearthed a Roman 'V' shaped ditch with fragments of Roman grey ware in it, such as was made at Wappenbury. This is believed to be either a Roman boundary ditch or one dug for a Roman marching camp. Sadly much of this area has been damaged by previous building work and we may never know the full story behind Coventry's first ever archaeologically excavated Roman ditch.
☛ *See* **LUNT**

RUDGE CYCLES

The first Rudge cycles were produced by Dan Rudge in his workshops in Wolverhampton. After his death the company was acquired by Mr George Woodcock, a businessman who changed its name to D Rudge & Co. and then the Coventry Tricycle Company, moving their best men and production to Spon Street. Over the following years the company's cycles won many championships, which stimulated sales and led to a need to expand into

The Rudge Cycle Works in 1898.

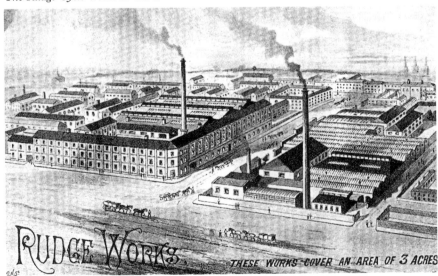

much bigger premises in Crow Lane. Expansion continued in 1885 when Woodcock made Rudge a limited company and introduced their own safety cycle, which became instantly popular. In 1888 the pneumatic tyre was introduced and the safety cycle took on its modern look. In 1889 the company won the International Gold Medal at the great exhibition in Paris. The company sold cycles to America, then France, until those countries copied the design and built their own. In 1891 George Woodcock died during a period of slackness in trade and the company began to falter. In 1896 the company became Rudge-Whitworth and things began to improve. Production grew from 1,216 cycles a week in June 1897 to a record 1,369 cycles in one day in 1905. The total cycle production for that year was 50,000 cycles, beaten the following year with the production of 75,000 Coventry-made cycles; Rudge-Whitworth had become the largest cycle manufacturer in the world.

RUPERT, PRINCE

Prince Rupert of the Rhine was the nephew of Charles I. Rupert attacked and burnt Birmingham with 2,000 men, probably cavalry, knowing that Birmingham men had helped to hold Coventry against his uncle the king. Birmingham was a fairly easy target as it had no wall to protect it. Rupert is quoted as saying at the time: 'Where's your Coventry now? Where's your God Brooke now?' Lord Brooke, parliamentarian general and Coventry's city recorder, had marched to Coventry's relief when the King had tried to gain entrance, forcing the King to drop his siege. Yet Coventry had not supplied men to protect Birmingham.

As Rupert passed by Coventry on 14 October 1642 he sent out a letter from the King, demanding again that the city be given up to the king, promising that the King would forget the past and the city would not be plundered. The city refused, saying they were 'forced to denye his Majesty's desires', because of the many inhuman acts of his Cavaliers. The next day Rupert's cavalry attacked, but quickly withdrew when they found twenty-six pieces of cannon playing upon them. They then rode off to fight at Edge Hill.

S

ST GEORGE

Coventry is the only place in England that claims to be the birthplace of St George. The church tradition is that he was born in Cappadocia but no one can prove it, hence the church demoted St George in recent years. In England in the early medieval period, the extremely pious Edward the Confessor was our unofficial national saint. England at this time was fighting France and St Edward just didn't spur on the English army into battle. Edward III therefore decided to create our own saint from an already existing one. A great warrior, leader of battle was chosen, namely St George – not however born in a foreign clime but in the centre of England, Caludon Castle hard by Coventry. St George became patron saint of England in 1349.

He was, we are told, the son of Lord Albert and before his birth his mother had a premonition that he would be a great champion and that she would die giving birth to him. Lord Albert sought the meaning of this from the enchantress Kalyb and on returning home found his wife dead and the child born bearing a birthmark of a dragon. During the darkness of night Kalyb stole the child and Lord Albert spent his last days searching for his son. Kalyb brought the child up in the lore of arms and at the age of 21 George decided he wanted to leave the enchantress. Kalyb offered him gifts if he would stay: invincible armour, Bayard the swiftest horse in the world and finally the magic sword Ascalon. George refused all, then using Kalyb's own wand, he entombed her in a cave in which she kept butchered babies. George then took the armour, sword and horse and rode off to free the then Six Champions of Christendom who had been magically imprisoned by the enchantress.

George returned to Coventry with the champions and here they honed their battle skills before riding south. At a golden pillar on Salisbury Plain they took seven roads to seven adventures. George fought his way across the Middle East and finally ended up in Egypt where he dispatched a dragon, two lions and a giant. There he won the heart of the Princess Sabra. He fought a war protecting Christianity and was crowned king of Egypt, emperor of Morocco and sultan of Persia. Then, as an ancient verse tells us:

> *Now it chanced at this*
> *time that St George he*
> *came home.*
> *To his dear lov'd*
> *Coventry: 'No more will*
> *I roam;*
> *I'll doff my stout*
> *armour, I'll sheath my*
> *brave sword*
> *And henceforth no more*
> *will I wander abroad.'*

On arriving back in his beloved Coventry with his princess George was informed that a dragon had been terrorizing the city. The great beast had emerged from the waters of Quinton Pool in Cheylesmore. The city fathers

Caludon Castle, the claimed birthplace of St George.

had been placating the beast by the traditional offering of a maiden left outside the 'Dragon's Gate' in Parkside. This area was pointed out in later years as having the claw marks of the dragon ripped into the stone. George would have none of this and strode forth and took on the great beast. We are told in verse that:

> *The dragon fared forth*
> *along the dark track,*
> *The dragon fared forth,*
> *but never fared back.*

George had done his work and Coventry was free from the terror. George then settled down in Coventry with the princess and had three strong sons. Other stories, however, say that the dragon came from a deep cavern under Hill Top and that George did not survive, dying from wounds sustained killing the beast. The people of Coventry are said to have buried him on what became St George's Day and built a chapel dedicated to him by his grave.

After his death he was said to be honoured yearly in Coventry with a procession called 'Riding the George' in which Coventry's saint would be accompanied by his princess and the dragon. St George's Day itself was marked by a major civic procession and the chapel of St George and a relic of George in the priory were the focus. Interestingly, Gosford Gate by St George's chapel had the blade bone of the giant boar which was slain by another local hero Sir Guy of Warwick, who was said locally to be the son of St George. Another building attached to the celebration was St Mary's Hall where in the fifteenth century a feast was held in his honour and his health drunk from a 'great standing cup of silver and gilt with the image of St George cut into it'.

Royalty often attended these processions, including Edward III, Henry V and Henry VI. Later in the seventeenth century St George led the Godiva procession through the streets of Coventry dressed in the black armour still to be seen in St Mary's Hall. The flower worn by the common people on St George's Day in the distant past was not the rose, which would not be in season. St George's flower was the bluebell which grew in proliferation during his feast, a true blue flower for a true blue saint.

ST JOHN THE BAPTIST

In 1344 during Queen Isabella's enforced retirement in Castle Rising, Norfolk, she wrote a letter to give to 'the good people of the Guild of St John the Baptist, in the town of Coventre, a piece of land called Babbelak, in the said town, in order that they may there build a chapel in honour of God and

The Church of St John the Baptist.

St John the Baptist'. Here they were to say prayers for the royal family and her late, murdered husband. The guild of St John amalgamated with St Mary's Guild, St Catherine's Guild and Trinity Guild and all together became the Trinity Guild which up until the Dissolution controlled the church. The small chapel was consecrated in 1350 and in 1357 William Walshman the Queen's valet gave more land and added a new aisle and more priests. Later the Black Prince gave another small plot to extend the building. Walshman continued to support the church, giving tenements to raise money for its upkeep. At times the church supported up to twelve priests who sang mass within its walls and lived in a building set within the quadrangle of the church. These priests also seem to have had an early school on this site.

The guild-run church continued until it was dissolved with Trinity Guild in 1547. The building then fell from use and had a mixed history thereafter. In 1647 Cromwell defeated the Scottish army at the Battle of Preston and a large number of prisoners found themselves kept within the walls of St John's. During their incarceration they did much damage, including smashing all the ancient stained glass. Over the following years the church was used as a store room, a stretch yard and many other things before being reopened as a parish church in 1734. As the church was built on oak piles on the site of a lake the area did suffer from occasional flooding. In December

1900 the inside of the church was flooded up to a height of five feet. Recent essential work to underpin the building showed that the church still stood on land with water only one foot below floor level.

☛ *See* SENT TO COVENTRY, QUEEN ISABELLA

ST MARY'S HALL

In 1340 a licence was given by Edward III to found a merchant guild in the city, under the name of the Guild of St Mary. The Guild Ordinance of 21 September 1342 states that the guild's annual meeting would be held on the Feast of the Assumption in the hall of Our Lady. So according to this, the first phase of St Mary's Hall was usable by 1342. The primary function of the guild was originally religious and charitable. The secondary reason, which soon became the prime function of the guild, was to look after the members' business interests. Within the following fifty years St Mary's Guild amalgamated with the guild of John the Baptist (with this guild came the chapel of St John in Fleet Street), St Catherine and the Trinity Guild. These united guilds became the all-powerful Guild of the Holy Trinity, St Mary, St John the Baptist and St Catherine, or more simply the Trinity Guild.

The Trinity Guild was confirmed in 1392 and in 1394 began to alter and extend the hall. The Trinity Guild became one of the most powerful guilds in the land and counted kings, princes and lords in its ranks. It was not however exclusively male-dominated, for amongst its ranks were 2,448 women, mainly of merchant status. Those who made up the guild were the most powerful in the city, so not surprisingly they also made up the city council, making St Mary's the seat of corporate power, with the Common Council meeting in the Great Hall and the inner council of twelve meeting in the Old Council Chamber. All of the guild masters had previously been mayors of the city. In fact, from the fourteenth century up until about three years ago, practically all of Coventry's mayor's were 'made' in the hall.

In its last years the Trinity Guild was joined by the city's second most powerful guild, the Guild of Corpus Christi. The newly empowered guild was not to last, for during the reign of Edward VI, in 1547, an Act of Confiscation was issued to all the merchant guilds in England. Their religious associations were used as a reason to dissolve them and acquire their lands and wealth and by Easter 1548 Edward had taken control of all the guild wealth in England. In 1552 St Mary's Hall was reacquired from the crown by the corporation and it reverted back to its previous use as a council house. Here the council continued to rule the city and in the reign of James I it became a closed, self-electing council and continued to be so until 1711. In that same year the mayor and council were accused of embezzling monies over £2,000 from the Thomas White Charity estate. To repay this the council sold the civic plate,

The north prospect of St Mary's Hall in Bayley Lane.

ST MARY'S HALL & OLD HOUSE

but could not raise enough and the hall was seized and lay out of civic hands for six years.

After its reacquisition the hall had a much more varied life as the more frugal council let it out as a venue for theatre, balls and general meetings and lectures. In 1824–6 the council restored the hall to its 'original' character; further restoration took place in 1834–5. The Old Council Chamber was used until the Municipal Corporation Act of 1835 and the hall still continued to play a major part in civic life until the building of the Council House in 1912–17. In October 1940 Caesar's Tower, the oldest standing structure in Coventry, was almost totally destroyed by a high-explosive bomb. In April 1941 the roof of the hall was badly burned by incendiaries and the hall suffered water damage. Both Caesar's Tower and the hall's roof were restored to their former glory and the hall continues to amaze people from across the globe.

St Mary's has had numerous notable visitors including Edward III, Edward IV, Henry V, Henry VI, Henry VII, James I, James II and Oliver Cromwell. It has also seen many literary figures, such as Charles Dickens, Jane Austen and Mary Ann Evans (George Eliot) to name a few. The latter based the courtroom scene from *Adam Bede* (published 1859) in St Mary's Hall:

> *The place fitted up that day as a court of justice was a grand old hall . . . The midday light that fell on the close pavement of human heads was shed through a line of high pointed windows, variegated with the mellow tints of old painted glass. Grim dusty armour hung in high relief in front of the dark oaken gallery at the farther end, and under the broad arch of the great mullioned window opposite was spread a curtain of old tapestry, covered with dim melancholy figures, like a dozing indistinct dream of the past. It was a place that through the rest of the year was haunted with the shadowy memories of old kings and queens, unhappy, discrowned, imprisoned . . .*

Mary Ann Evans may have witnessed a real trial here for the hall was used as a courtroom in the late seventeenth to early eighteenth centuries and the late eighteenth to early nineteenth centuries. Another writer who used the hall in a novel was A E Mason.

Perhaps one of the most famed visitors to St Mary's was William Shakespeare, for the companies with which he toured played the hall on numerous occasions. Another association with Shakespeare is the ancient oak table in the Old Council Chamber, which was acquired from Lord Lucy of Charlecote in 1902 with an attached tradition that this was the table on which Shakespeare's arrest warrant was signed for sheep stealing. Shakespeare ran away and eventually turned up in London – and the rest, as they say, is history.

In January 1940, with the threat of war, the Coventry Tapestry was taken down and removed to Keresley Colliery for safety. At the same time the glass was taken out of the Great Hall and great chair and other pieces crated and placed for safety at the bottom of Caesar's Tower. In October 1940 the tower was hit by a single high-explosive bomb which almost completely demolished the ancient tower, but the objects stored in its base survived – although some, like the Great Chest, were blown apart. All was restored and it is now impossible to tell that the objects suffered. It appears that the roof bosses were left in situ, as were the paintings and armour. On 8 April 1941 during a heavy raid the hall's roof was partially burnt by incendiary bombs. The water used to fight the fire caused some damage to the paintings and the armour was reported as damaged. The south end of the hall had extensive water damage, with the walls blackened. Shortly afterwards the hall's roof was covered with corrugated iron, with wooden boards on top. In 1943 the hall was used for three months to issue ID cards and ration books. The hall is now open to visitors.

ST MICHAEL'S (OLD CATHEDRAL)

The first mention we appear to have of the church of St Michael, then a chapel, is in the Langley Cartulary which refers to the chapel as being 'in ballivo qui ducit ad ecclesiam sancti Michaelis', or the church of St Michael in the bailey. This refers to the chapel lying within the bailey of Coventry Castle. It lay on the south side of the bailey against the ditch which still runs through the centre of the present church. This chapel was built for the use of Ranulf, earl of Chester, when he was in residence. Later Ranulf gave all the chapels he built around the district, including that of St Michael, into the hands of Prior Laurence of Coventry Priory. There was later some argument over the chapel and the bishop of Coventry, Geoffrey de Muschamp, claimed control over the building. The first vicar of this church chosen by the earl and bishop was one Ralph de Maynwaring. At this time Prior Laurence renounced his claim on the chapel, but the priory didn't give up the fight for this church and its chapels which brought in a considerable sum of money, and in 1248 it reacquired them on the death of the existing priests.

In 1249 St Michael's chapel was first constituted a church. Over the following years buildings and land were gifted to help build the church and the building began to grow. The rebuilding and enlarging of the church, with its tower, octagon and spire, appears to date mainly from 1400 to 1450. The choir and chancel date from an earlier period. The church was unable to expand towards the south due to the proximity of St Mary's Hall.

One of the greatest moments in the church's history was when mass was held here for Henry VI and his queen, Margaret of Anjou, in 1451. It is

The interior of St Michael's church photographed the year before its destruction.

recorded that on the day of the mass Henry led a royal procession of high clergy, lords and ladies from the priory to St Michael's and there celebrated mass conducted by his uncle Cardinal Beaufort. Some sources have said that this is the event celebrated on the Coventry Tapestry in St Mary's Hall. After mass Henry presented the church with his gown of gold tissue and sable. It has been suggested that this event was held to mark the end of the great rebuilding of the church, the last phase being the new west entrance especially created for the King to pass through.

In 1522 the vicar of St Michael's was still being selected by the prior and the church maintained many chapel and chantries, employing eighteen priests and six chantry priests. In 1553, with the Reformation, the last of these priests were pensioned off. In the early 1600s Puritans were the ruling elite in Coventry; however, in 1633, beliefs were dominated by Archbishop Laud and his lead was followed by the council. The Revd William Panting, an Anglican, was made vicar of St Michael's. Panting tried to force the Puritan congregation to follow Laud but they were mainly against it. In 1642 the Puritans held sway again and Panting and his Laudian beliefs were replaced by the Revd Obadiah Grew, who remained in post until the Restoration forced him to resign his benefice. He continued to preach but later had to leave. He did return, as he still held a licence to preach, but in 1682 his licence was revoked by James II and Grew found himself in

Coventry Gaol for six months. He was again forced to leave but returned to preach again after the 'Glorious Revolution' and continued to do so until a month before his death, aged 82, in 1689.

Over the next centuries St Michael's settled down into a normal life of worship. The building itself received attention between 1883 and 1890, when major restoration work was done, including a complete resurfacing of the tower and octagon. St Michael's, claimed to be the largest parish church in England, was made a cathedral in 1918 and its first bishop was Yeatman-Biggs. As a cathedral it lasted twenty-two years, for on the night of 14 November 1940 the cathedral was fire-bombed and completely burned out. After its destruction many called for its rebuilding but the decision was made to build a new cathedral, also dedicated to St Michael.

ST MICHAEL'S CATHEDRAL

Within a year of the destruction of the Old Cathedral, as it became known, a commission sat to discuss the possibility of rebuilding. Many wanted the old church restored but the commission chose to ask Sir Giles Gilbert Scott to submit a new design for a new cathedral. His design to build a new cathedral on the site of the old, with a central altar, was approved by the Church Commissioners but turned down by the Royal Fine Arts Commission. Scott withdrew his design and in 1950 the council decided to hold an open competition, receiving 219 entries from across the globe. Many of these, like Scott's, proposed to demolish the ruins of the old cathedral.

The winner was announced in August 1951 as Basil Spence, who envisaged a new cathedral attached to the old. He claimed it had come to him as a vision in the summer of 1950 when he had visited the ruins and within twenty-four hours he had created his design. When his plans were published Spence received 700 letters, mainly telling him how horrible the design was. Because of the

The New Cathedral with Epstein's St Michael and the Devil.

publicity commissions began to dry up and no work materialized over the following two years, bringing Spence to the verge of bankruptcy.

Work began on the building and Spence chose the best materials and the best artists of the day to fill his vision. Graham Sutherland was commissioned to create the largest tapestry in the world using 12,000 miles of wool. John Hutton created the great glass west screen covered in saints and angels, under which his ashes now lie. John Piper and Patrick Reyntiens created the baptistery windows and Jacob Epstein the huge bronze *St Michael and the Devil*. In total the building cost £1,385,000 and was dedicated by the Queen on 25 May 1962. In the first year the building received two and a half million visitors and is still today one of the most visited buildings in England. The cathedral became a centre for world reconciliation and in 1999 was voted one of Britain's best loved buildings. Basil Spence was knighted for his work.

ST NICHOLAS

The church of St Nicholas stood off St Nicholas Street, Radford. Its dedication to St Nicholas is suggestive that its establishment may have been very early. The church, which unusually appeared to have a tower and spire at each end, may have been Coventry's oldest church, possibly even the church believed to have been set up here in the seventh century by St Chad. Considering the fact that it existed until the sixteenth century, very little is known about the church. It was maintained by the guilds of Corpus Christi and St Nicholas and at one time maintained fifteen chaplains. It appears to have been badly affected by the dissolution of the guilds in 1547. Thereafter the towers and spires were demolished and it was apparently used as a barn until it fell into complete ruin and disappeared over the following 100 years. The church itself later was only recalled through the field names, 'Little' and 'Big' Steeple Fields.

SCOTS, MARY, QUEEN OF

On the night of 25 November 1569 Mary, Queen of Scots, with her fifty servants, escorted by the earls of Huntingdon and Shrewsbury and 400 troops, entered the city. She was placed in the city's largest inn, the Bull in Smithford Street. Mary and her retinue filled the inn, leaving no room for the earls. Huntingdon wrote: 'She lieth at an inn, where for me there is no lodging; her men also lie in the town, and go where they will.' Incensed Elizabeth wrote back saying Mary should not lie at a 'common' inn but somewhere more suitable and secure, such as Hale's house (Whitefriars) where she herself had stayed. The earl wrote back saying that Hales's house was not available and they were looking for somewhere else.

About a week later they informed the Queen that they had moved her, but mentioned that the new accommodation suffers from 'straightness of room', meaning it had little domestic furniture. One version of the city annals tells us that the Scottish queen was placed in the Old Mayoress's Parlour which is the present Draper's Room in St Mary's Hall. The following day she and her retinue were moved again, this time to the 'former lord chief baron's house', Whitefriars, where she stayed until 2 January.

While in Coventry Mary was frequently visited by Henry Goodere, who back in May 1568 had devised a secret code for her to use when writing to her friends. Goodere of Polesworth Hall also had a house in Much Park Street where the Warwickshire poet Michael Drayton, a friend of Shakespeare, was

Mary, Queen of Scots.

employed. For his help Mary presented him with a gift of gold buttons. Elizabeth, however, in September 1571, put him in the Tower for 'unlawful dealing touchinge the Q. of Scoots'. He was later forgiven by Queen Elizabeth who in 1599 knighted him.

Since the middle of the nineteenth century it has been claimed that Mary was held in a small cell-like room in Caesar's Tower at the back of St Mary's Hall. This story was no doubt made up, along with other stories at that time, for its inventor had little knowledge of history and assumed Mary was a prisoner in the normal sense, hence the tiny cell-like room. Mary was never kept in cells, only whole buildings or wings of large houses. She had her retinue of fifty servants to house too.

The Coventry antiquarian William Humberstone wrote in the *Coventry Herald* as far back as 1919: 'There is an old stately chamber known as the Mayoress's Parlour . . . and this is no doubt the apartment referred to [in the annals]. A worst blunder is that which assigns a gloomy prison-like room, still popularly known as Queen Mary's Chamber.'

SEIGE OF COVENTRY

During its long history Coventry has seen a number of sieges; King Stephen placed Coventry Castle under siege. In the past at least five huge stone trebuchet balls have been unearthed in the city centre, thrown into the walled city by massive siege engines, in some unspecified time. During the fifteenth century King Edward IV, with an army of 30,000, twice encamped outside the city demanding battle from the earl of Warwick who was ensconced within its walls. The city's most famous siege, however, took place in the seventeenth century as England collapsed into civil war. King Charles arrived at Stoneleigh Abbey and from there declared his intention to visit Coventry. The royal herald, William Dugdale, was sent to the city to inform them and was told that the King's army would not be welcome – only he and 200 of his cavaliers would be allowed to enter the city. Meanwhile the earl of Northampton no doubt came to the king via Coventry and informed him of the position there relating to troops and the general feeling in the city which did not favour the royal forces. After Dugdale returned and informed the King of Coventry's answer the King wrote a summons threatening devastation:

Charles R

Whereas divers persons ill affected to his Matie's person and government, and strangers to his Cittie of Coventry, are lately gotten into that Cittie with armes and munic'on, who, with others of that place ill affected to the peace of this his Kingdome, have combined to keepe the said Cittie by force of armes against his Matie, their Leige Lord and Soverein; for reducing of whom to their obedience his Matie hath given orders to some Com'anders of the Forces to assault the said Cittie, and by force to enter the same.

Notwithstanding, his Matie being verie unwilling for some disaffected persons to punish his good subjects and ruine his said Cittie, is graciously pleased thereby to declare. That in case the said Strangers shall forthwith, after the publishing of this His Proclamac'on, depart peaceably out of the said Cittie, and they and the Inhabitants presently lay down their armes, that then his Matie will pardon as well all the said Strangers, as all other the Inhabitants of the said Cittie.

But if they persist in their said Acc'on of Rebellion, then his Matie is resolved to proceed against them as Traytors and Rebells, and to use all extremity for reducing the said Cittie to due obedience.

Given at our Court of Stonely Abby the twentieth day of August, in the eighteen year of or Reigne, 1642.

The earliest printed document relating to the siege itself was written and printed on 25 August 1642 while the siege was still under way: *The King's Maiesties Alarum for Open War*. The *Alarum* states that:

His Majesty out of high indignation of his supposed injuries, being full and confident in his own cause, hath with eleven thousand men strongly besieged the City of Coventry, and environed them so strongly, that there is no way possible for them to escape, unless that they betimes allay the indignation of the Kings designes, which are hitherto so violent, that he intends to make their City the object of the thundering Canon, and that their houses shall be beaten down about their eares for their opposing of his Majesty, in refusing to give him admittance into their City. With these and such like comminations and threatenings the people are much disheartened and affrighted, and to increase their fears, together with the whole Kingdomes, the King's Majesty hath commanded his subjects on the North side of the Trent, and all places adjoining within twenty miles Southward thereof, on the obligation of their allegiance, to attend his Royall Person upon Munday being the two and twentieth day of this moneth of August at Dunsmore Heath, where his Majesty intends to erect his Standard Royall . . .

King Charles I laid his cannon against the city.

The *Alarum* states that Charles had with him 11,000 foot and 6,000 horse and forty-six cannon set against the city. The fact that the King, now unable to gain entrance into Coventry, was intending to raise his standard on Dunsmore Heath shows that almost certainly his original intention was to officially begin the war from Coventry. Soon after this report, the King heard of the approach of Coventry's recorder, the earl of Essex, with his army, forcing him to abandon the siege and head north where he would finally fly his 'Standard Royall' at Nottingham and thus officially begin the war.

SENT TO COVENTRY

Most people assume that they know where the saying 'sent to Coventry' originated: in the seventeenth century Royalist soldiers were imprisoned in St John's church and when they exercised in the street the populace shunned them, hence the saying. Unfortunately part of this explanation only appears to date from the 1930s when city clerk Frederick Smith put it in his city guide and later in 1947 in his book *Six Hundred Years of Municipal Life*. The connection to St John's first appears in the 1950s. Only one historian, Hutton, who wrote a *History of Birmingham*, links the phrase to the Civil War, saying that occasionally troublesome royalist prisoners were sent from Birmingham to Coventry and were scorned in the city. He may have taken this from Clarendon's *History of the Rebellion*, written well over a century earlier, which states: 'At Bromingham a town so generally wicked that it has risen upon small parties of the King's and killed or taken them prisoners and sent them to Coventry.' Clarendon was in fact only saying that prisoners were being sent to Coventry, which was so, but makes no mention of the saying.

Grose, in his *Classical Dictionary of the English Tongue*, published in 1785, gives another reason, looking for the first time at the actual saying itself. It relates to Coventry being a garrison town:

> *To send one to Coventry, a punishment inflicted by officers of the army on such of their brethren as are testy, or have been guilty of improper behaviour not worthy the cognizance of a court martial. The person sent to Coventry is considered as absent; no one may speak to him, or answer any question he asks, except relative to duty, under penalty of him being sent to the same place. On a proper submission the penitent is recalled, and welcomed by the mess as just returned from a journey to Coventry.*

The saying became widespread and in 1779 the Revd James Woodforde wrote in his diary: 'We laughed immoderately after dinner on Mrs Howes being sent to Coventry by us for an Hour.' In 1869 Benjamin Poole wrote in his *History and Antiquities of Coventry*:

> *In former times the principal inhabitants of Coventry had a strong antipathy to association with soldiers. If a female, especially was known to hold any conversation with anyone holding a military commission, she immediately became the object of popular scandal. With the military therefore, who were the subject of this prejudice ... and consequently found themselves, as it were isolated, and confined to their own quarters and mess rooms ... meaning thereby, that to send a man to Coventry was to exclude him from all ordinary intercourse with society and condemn him to a comparatively solitary life.*

In 1888 T W Whitley wrote, 'The Barracks reminds one that the origin of the phrase, "Sent to Coventry" probably arose from the boycotting used towards military men. At that period the people seemed to think association with soldiers was a thing to be avoided, and no decent citizen spoke to them.' The people of Coventry certainly at times did have reasons to dislike the soldiers based within the city, for occasionally soldiers were known to kill unarmed citizens during drunken arguments. Soldiers were also used to quell the mob at times of trouble and even during food shortages. During these events sometimes troops got heavy-handed and people were seriously injured. Such occasions were not forgotten by the citizens who were wary of the troops amongst them. Then there was of course their fraternizing with young ladies and the possible consequences. Not surprisingly people avoided fraternizing with the troops. However, the historian Benjamin Poole wrote, in the 1860s: 'It is unnecessary to add that no such ground for complaint against Coventry exists any longer.'

SHAKESPEARE, WILLIAM

The first mention of a Shakespeare in Warwickshire was in 1358 when Thomas Shakespeare, a mercer, killed a goldsmith in Coventry by striking him on the head with his sword. An inquest followed and Thomas Shakespeare's goods, valued at 2 shillings were confiscated, but Shakespeare had fled and was presumably outlawed. As for the Bard himself, it is believed as a young man Shakespeare witnessed the Mystery Plays for he later mentions its notable raving Herod and the Devil which dragged unsuspecting individuals into hell. William Shakespeare actually played Coventry with the Queen's Men every year from 1585 to 1591. By itself this could   amount to up to sixty performances. In 1594 he joined the Chamberlains Men who again played Coventry. His last tour as a player was with the King's Men who played the city in 1603. It seems likely that, on all these occasions, Shakespeare played St Mary's

William Shakespeare.

Hall as it was normal to put on the 'Mayor's Play' first for the mayor who would say yea or nay as to whether it continued in the venue.

SHELTON, JOHN BAILEY

Known deservedly as the 'Father of Coventry's Archaeology', John Bailey Shelton, or 'JB' as he was affectionately known, single-handedly laid the foundation of Coventry's archaeological collection. JB explored every building site and bomb crater in the city from the 1930s until his death, when he was hit by a motorcycle in 1958. Although JB didn't keep records in the modern sense he did record some of his digs in articles he penned for *Austin's Monthly Magazines*, he also kept other records, which were sadly destroyed in the blitz. JB first got interested in archaeology in 1927 when he was in hospital with four fractures to his leg. During this time he was reading about old Coventry and when he returned home he hobbled on crutches to where workmen were working on the Hare and Squirrel and got permission to excavate. Here he uncovered a four foot thick wall, a column and encaustic tiles. JB believed this was the site of a chapel built by the Greyfriars.

In 1937 JB wrote of finding the water which fed the priory and its mill, saying: 'Somewhere beneath the hill between the Meadow and Priory Row is a spring of clear and swift flowing water which supplied the power for driving the mill wheel.' He later unearthed a 'pipe' carrying the water; it was cut from tree trunks with plank tops pegged to the bottom. JB carefully removed a plank and revealed, 'the swift flowing water from the spring in the hill' still flowing as it had for centuries. In July 1937 JB opened his own museum at his home 69 Little Park Street and called it the 'Benedictine Museum'. Here he displayed over 2,000 objects which he had personally rescued in the city during his many digs and explorations.

During the blitz John's home in Little Park Street was destroyed by fire. He fought that night between bomb blast and fire to save his many horses, for which he later received the Queen Victoria Medal from the RSPCA. John and his wife afterwards lived in a caravan on a bombsite in Little Park Street. Around this time JB also looked after St Mary's Hall, showing it to visitors, and was given the title of city chamberlain in respect for the position he held not only in the hall but also in the city. In 1956 JB received an MBE for his years of public service and dedication to the people and history of Coventry.

JB was not born in Coventry but in Kirby Woodhouse in Nottinghamshire in 1875, the son of a farm labourer. Why he came to Coventry we are not sure, but it may have been through his connection to the Wesleyans of Kirby and Coventry. When he came to Coventry he started as a railway drayman, then developed his own carting business. It is certain that Coventry in many ways was made richer by his presence.

SHERBOURNE

The river which flows through Coventry is called the Sherbourne, deriving its name from the Anglo-Saxon meaning 'clear' or 'shining' stream. The river is special, for its source rises from the ground and can be found north of Coventry between two fields near Belcher Wood, by Bridle Brook Lane, close to Corley Moor. Rivers that came from the ground were always considered by our ancestors to have some sacred significance. In fact, the appellation of shining may refer to its sacredness. The earlier name for the river appears to be 'Cune', which can be found in the Celtic language referring to the water god Condatis or from the word 'Cune' meaning Hound, the River of the Hound. This of course could suggest that the river was a boundary to a Celtic chief's land. Interestingly, in the north of Coventry we also have a Hounds Hill, or Cune Barr, the hill of the hound. The area also contains other surviving words from the Celtic language such as 'Hen' Lane (the Old Lane) and the archaic 'Wyblino' stream. The Cune in fact passes through Coundon, an area which once had an Iron Age site and was the findspot of a harness fitting from a horse which once pulled a Celtic chariot, a high-status vehicle.

SIDDONS, SARAH

Sarah Siddons was England's finest eighteenth-century actress and she has strong connections with the city. During the late eighteenth century the actress with various companies played Coventry on many occasions at St Mary's Hall and the nearby Draper's Hall. In 1773 the company of her father Roger Kemble was playing at the Draper's Hall. Sarah Kemble had formed an attachment with fellow actor and company member William Siddons. Her father had forbidden her to have a relationship with an actor and sacked Siddons from the company. Afterwards, to keep her occupied and out of the way, he obtained a position for Sarah as a companion or maid to Lady Greatheed of Guy's Cliff House, near Warwick.

The ploy failed and on 25 November 1773 18-year-old Sarah Kemble married William Siddons by licence at Holy Trinity church. The ceremony was attended by the entire cast and the marriage certificate was signed

An eighteenth-century portrait of the actress Sarah Siddons.

by her father. The marriage was performed by a stand-in, George Richards, as the then vicar, Joseph Rann, though he had produced a folio of Shakespeare's works had no time for lowly touring actors. Sarah had talked her father into the marriage. A story says that when her father forbade her to marry Siddons, an actor, her response was that you could hardly call him an actor and indeed he wasn't, not compared with this giantess of the Georgian stage. Unfortunately their marriage wasn't a success, despite five children, and the couple gradually drifted apart. In June 1805, under her old name of Mrs Kemble, she performed to a packed audience at St Mary's Hall the part of Lady Teazle in Sheriden's *School for Scandal*. Sarah continued to act and visit her friends in Coventry and Guy's Cliff, where she was entertained now as an honoured guest. She died in 1831, mourned by a nation.

SOLDIERS

Before Coventry Barracks was built in 1793 Coventry had been a garrison city with troops stationed here on a regular basis. General Wade's Regiment was stationed in the city in 1746, while en route to Scotland. In 1756 General Steuart's Regiment was quartered in the city. It was written of that particular regiment at the time that 'A gunsmith who had examined several of their firelocks declared t'other day that they were so crooked in the barrels that if you was to shoot a ball out of them upon a line, before it flew two hundred yards it would enter the earth, and he believed that the firelocks of the whole regiment were the same.'

The presence of soldiers in the city often resulted in conflicts with locals, leading to them to being shunned by the populace. The *Coventry Mercury* reported in 1757:

At a public house in this city on Saturday night last an fray happened between a soldier and two other men, in which the soldier cut one of them with a hanger [slightly curved single-edged sword] in the face, in so desperate a manner that his life is despaired of. The watchmen coming in, the soldier struck at 'em and accidentally cut off one of his fingers. He has since been taken into custody.

A mid-eighteenth-century foot soldier.

Another incident with a bayonet led to a local farmer's death and the soldier in question escaped imprisonment. Other soldiers were punished for various military offences. In April 1757 the *Mercury* reported: 'On Saturday last, about noon, a soldier belonging to General Steuart's Regiment, quartered in the city, was shot for desertion, in the Park. He had been condemned to be shot for desertion once before and was reprieved. He behaved very penitent, and acknowledged he deserved to die.' In June another soldier named George Robinson was shot in the park. Described as an 'old offender', Robinson died very penitent, blaming his downfall on loose women. Others who had simply deserted, quite a common occurrence in the British army in the eighteenth and nineteenth centuries, suffered a lesser fate. One such man in Steuart's Regiment was taken to the park, given one thousand lashes and drummed out of the regiment with a halter about his neck. The site where the men were executed and punished was by a small projection in the city wall which stood behind the present police headquarters in Little Park Street.

A soldier's grave can still be seen in St Michael's churchyard, lying flat before the County Hall. It had on it a crossed pistol, carbine and hanger and the following words:

> *Sacred*
> *To the memory of*
> *Daniel John Hanley*
> *Late Corporal 14th Kings*
> *Light Dragoons*
> *Who died Feb.y 3 1839*
> *Aged 20*
> *When the last trumpets*
> *awful voice*
> *This rendering earth shall*
> *Shake*
> *Then opening graves shall*
> *yield, then charge*
> *And dust to life awake*
> *This stone was erected by his brother non*
> *commissioned officers as a tribute of sincere respect.*

Hanley's fellow Light Dragoons would have made a splendid and colourful sight as they practised their martial skills with sword and lance on Greyfriars Green, much to the admiration of the young ladies. The dragoons, however, were also used to suppress public protests and more than once they were set against the people. Sometimes the sight of them was enough, if not the sabres would actually be used to attack Coventry citizens. Another dragoon who saw service in the Crimea then died of an unspecified illness in Coventry was commemorated in the Mercers Chapel by the west door. His monument read:

Sacred to the memory of Joseph Massey O'Keeffe of the 4th Irish Dragoon Guards who died in Coventry, June 1st, 1861, aged 36 years. The deceased served in the Regiment for upwards of 18 years and was with it in the Crimean War of 1854 and 1855, including the battles of Balaclava, Inkerman, the Tchernaya, and the siege and taking of Sebastopol.

This tablet is erected by the Officers, Non Commissioned Officers, and Men of his (F) troop, to the memory of a true comrade, and a good soldier.

Other soldiers didn't stay in the city because they died, but because they married. My own great-grandfather was one such man, coming to Coventry with the Royal Artillery after the Egyptian War in 1882. His wife's father, my great-great-grandfather, was one of the city's few Chelsea Out Pensioners. Born in Coventry in 1808 he served in the 60th Rifles as colour sergeant then as colour sergeant of the Warwickshire Militia for over fifty years.

☛ *See* **BARRACKS, SENT TO COVENTRY**

STOCKS

The stocks were a favoured form of punishment for centuries for petty offenders. Coventry had numerous sets of stocks scattered around the city to accommodate them. The city Leet Book tells of the following places where stocks could be found in the fifteenth and sixteenth centuries: Mill Lane, Bishop Gate, Well Street Gate, New Street, Greyfriars Gate, Little Park Street Gate, New Gate and a set just beyond the chapel of St Christopher and St James in Spon Street and sets at Bablake and St George's chapel in Gosford Street. In 1574 it was also recorded that a set of stocks stood in the churchyard shared by Holy Trinity and St Michael. In 1575 the Leet Book notes a set of new stocks erected in Cross Cheaping next to the cage, which was a tall narrow cage about 6 feet tall which was pivoted and could be made to spin around by passers-by, making the incarcerated felon sick. In 1583 a new set of stocks was erected in the Bull Ring at the bottom of Butcher Row.

Another new set was erected in 1619 in Vicar Lane, off Smithford Street. These were later moved to the Market Square and placed outside the Watch House, known as the 'Bog House Prison', a smelly holding house used by the city watchmen. In the nineteenth century these particular stocks had certain regulars, usually drunks such as ribbon weaver George 'Trodge' Chittem. Trodge was particularly effective at taking off his boots and slipping out of the stocks for a quick pint in the Spread Eagle which stood but a few feet away. If he was invited for a drink and the constable was present Trodge would say, 'Don't be a fool, you know I can't come.' In fact, Trodge Chittem spent so long in the stocks he began to refer to himself as the 'Master of the Stocks'.

A man who disputed this title was watchmaker Charlie Kirk, who had started life as a successful watch engraver but developed a fondness for the drink. When locked up in the stocks Kirk often bring his work with him and sit engraving his watch cocks. He also seemed to have a way of entertaining the crowd that gathered around him. Kirk hadn't developed the skill of slipping out of the stocks but like most others would lean back against the nearby window and call out 'May I?' If the watchman was in a good mood he

The stocks frequented by George Chittem photographed in the 1860s outside the Watch House.

would release the prisoner and accompany him to the Spread Eagle for a pint. If the watchman didn't want to go, the prisoner would be allowed to go on his own, as long as he didn't stay too long. Those who did were reminded of where they should be and the usual retort was: 'I'm coming, I'm coming. Don't worrit me so. Give a chap a chance to empty his mug.'

It is said that during the later years the stocks became easier to get out of as the holes were worn, as was the lock and clasp. With the final closure of Coventry Gaol came the closure of the Watch House and the stocks were afterwards re-erected under the oriel window of St Mary's Hall. They were, however, at this time purely ornamental. They were later stored under the hall and are now kept at Coventry's Art Gallery and Museum.

Other seventeenth-century stocks were erected by the Gaol Hall near the corner of Pepper (then Gaol) Lane and Cuckoo Lane. From 1640 is the following pricing for the repair of a set of stocks: 'Paid for making new irons for the stocks at the Bull Ring, which the Souldiers broke and took away, weighing 36 lbs, and crab nails, iiijs [4 shillings].'

STODDART, ANDREW ERNEST

Andrew Ernest Stoddart became captain of England in both cricket and rugby. He was a team mate of W G Grace and a national sporting hero, having led England in a victory over Australia in 1894–5. Stod or Stoddie, as he was affectionately known, scored 352 runs in the Test and toured Australia four times, and the West Indies and America. Stoddie also played rugby and won ten England caps. In later years he struggled with his health and in 1915 aged 52 he committed suicide by shooting himself in the head with a revolver. He was not Coventry-born but his mother had lived with his sister in Sandy Lane, Radford, for a number of years and 'Our dear victorious Stod' as he was known was buried with his mother in St Nicholas churchyard, Radford. In November 1940 his grave was destroyed with the church when a single landmine flattened the site.

SWANSWELL POOL

Up to the seventeenth century, the pool, originally part of the great Bablake, was called the 'Swineswell'. Legend states that it got its name from a giant boar that rutted here in the distant past. The giant beast's snout and tusks ripped up the ground, making a huge hole which after being filled by a local stream nicknamed the 'Severn' and the many springs in the area, formed the pool we know today. The monstrous boar's rutting not surprisingly terrorized the people of Coventry until Sir Guy of Warwick came along and dispatched it. For centuries afterwards a great bone claimed to be from the beast (or others say the Dun Cow) hung on Gosford Gate. The bone was symbolically cast back into the Swanswell in the mid-nineteenth century.

In 1632 the spring that helped to feed the pool became Coventry's first city centre waterworks. Here Bartholomew Bewdley, a plumber, and stone mason Thomas Sargeson built a conduit which, using a hydraulic engine, forced the water uphill through lead pipes to a small reservoir which stood in Cuckoo Lane near the present Coventry Cross. These waterworks were still in use up until 1846.

A late nineteenth-century reminiscence of the area says:

Swanswell Fields, too were rich with waving corn, and had two pools of water of much greater area than the present pond, and that portion of the district around the pools, which was not cultivated, formed a rank and secluded marsh where wild fowl sported amongst the tall reeds and rushes.

The writer and artisan William Gutteridge added:

The low ground immediately surrounding the pool was covered with extensive osier and reed beds. This place was the favourite resort and breeding place of several kinds of waterfowl. The wild duck, the widgeon, the dipper and the water hen were constant visitors, and the reeds and osiers beds were enlivened by the songs of the warblers that abounded. The water itself teemed with fish, as it does to this day. Pike, perch, roach, tench and eels afforded fine sport for anglers. Before the New Town of Hill Fields encroached upon the pool it was a wild and weird place. The water was bordered with fine old pollard willows . . . The view of the pool was almost obscured in the narrow causeway by the willows and clusters of tall elms, oaks, chestnuts, and maples that surrounded it.

Around this period the Swanswell was cut down in size and a small pool next to it disappeared. William Odell wrote in the late nineteenth century:

Of Swanswell Pools, for there were two, about 1850 the smaller one was filled up, and the large one much reduced in size, so as to allow of a street being made in front of it, leading from Cook Street Gate to St Peter's Church, which till then was only a narrow footway. Opposite the pool and by the side of the footway stood an old fashioned stone house, with a porch . . . I was told that the Bewley's a respectable family formerly lived there.

This house stood next to the waterworks and Richard Jeliffe wrote in the nineteenth century that 'Madame Bewley lived at the waterworks old house.'

SWANSWELL SPRING

By the side of Swanswell Pool for many centuries could be found the Swanswell Spring, which was noted for the purity of its water. It was to be found by the side of a narrow highway leading from Swanswell to Mill Lane and was approached by steps from the pathway. It stood in 'rustic surroundings', with the water pouring forth from a metal spout. Here it was said from time immemorial large numbers of Coventry men went for their morning wash as the water was valued so highly. The popular pure spring disappeared when Cox Street was made.

Before White Street was built there also existed a little round building by the pool which contained a plunge bath fed by spring water. The Swanswell area down to St Agnes Lane was once noted for its fine springs. St Agnes Lane itself took its name from another spring-fed rustic stone trough called St Agnes's Well, the water of which was later utilized by Lant's who made pop.

T

TERRY, ELLEN

Dame Ellen Terry, England's most famed nineteenth/twentieth-century Shakespearean actress was born in Market Street, Coventry, on 27 February 1848. Her birth occurred in the city as her parents both jobbing actors were playing a local theatre. Soon after her birth the company and the Terrys moved on. Her birthplace was said to be Market Street, although her birth certificate says Smithford Street. This may be simply because the part of Market Street coming off Smithford Street didn't have a set name in the year of her birth. Two buildings opposite each other both held rival claims to be the birthplace of the great actress: a tripe shop was the favourite but when asked on a visit to Coventry Dame Ellen could not be sure.

Dame Ellen Terry, Coventry born, but not bred.

THORNTON, JOHN

John Thornton was in the early fifteenth century England's greatest stained-glass artist. His work was at least a hundred years ahead of its time; while others produced two-dimensional figures in glass Thornton's were three-dimensional, with effective use of shading. It is believed that, although his work appeared all over the country, the actual work on the creation of the glass pieces which make up the windows was done in his Coventry workshop in the Burges (St John's Bridges). That said, his greatest work, the Great East Window at York Minister, which is said to contain more stained glass than any other window in England, was produced while he was in residence in York and was completed in 1405. The indenture between John Thornton of Coventry and the dean and chapter of York still survives and states:

The artist is to complete it in three years, portray with his own hands the histories, images, and other things, to be painted on the same, to provide glass, and lead, and workmen and receive four shillings per week, five pounds at the end of each year, and after the work is complete ten pounds for his reward.

To see how valued Thornton was as a stained-glass artist he can be compared to another glazier John Burgh who worked on York Minister in 1400. He received but one penny a day for his work. Thornton was made a freeman of York in 1410 and retained a property in the city. The following year he is recorded as being back in Coventry living in the Burges. He was still living in the Burges in 1430 when he paid 5 shillings towards a loan to King Henry VI.

U

UNIONS

It appears that there was some trade union activity in Coventry as early as 1730. The way these groups conducted themselves could be considered questionable by modern standards. In issue 46 of the *Grub Street Journal*, dated 19 November 1730, we find a copy of a letter which was said to have been secretly put under a master weaver's door and believed to be a direct threat from a union. It reads:

Friend Towers
By these we let you understand that we are a body of men that have considered the distress of the poor Weavers, and are firmly bound by oath upon pain of death to have the burden of these poor suffers eased, by raising the prices of all sorts of work twelve pence per piece. But upon the refusal of the request your house shall be laid in ashes, at a time when your bodies shall have much ado to escape, for

Members of the United Machine Workers Association probably taking part in a Godiva procession

you are a sort of men that delight to grind the face of the poor. It will be justice to execute the greatest judgement upon you, and not on you only, but upon all Master Weavers in general.

I cannot but be loyal to Government. God save the King.

I cannot say whether this threat was carried out or not, but by the early nineteenth century some things hadn't improved. When ribbon manufacturer James Beck introduced the first steam-powered looms into his workshop in Beck's Yard, off New Buildings, unionists had a meeting concerning it in Broadgate and afterwards the crowd attacked Beck's 'factory' and burnt it to the ground. Beck himself narrowly escaped with his life and there were threats to hang him or beat him to death. The mob was finally brought under control when the cavalry came out of the barracks. Certain union members were at first condemned to death but later their sentences were changed to transportation. James Beck died a pauper and one of his transported attackers latter returned from Australia a rich man.

The *Coventry Herald and Observer* reported in March 1834 an extraordinary funeral showing the following of some unions in nineteenth-century Coventry:

On Tuesday last the funeral of Mr Pearson took place, in the burying ground of the Independent Chapel, Foleshill. The deceased was a leading member of the Trades Union, and was buried with a ceremony peculiar to the Order. The procession consisted of about fifteen hundred persons, partly women who were arrayed in white and wearing hoods. A number of men, who we understand to be officers of the Union, were dressed in gowns. By one of these was carried the Bible on a cushion, the Wardens carrying battle axes, made of wood, and the Tyler's their drawn swords ... the funeral excited considerable interest, and was witnessed by several thousand spectators.

Unions covered all types of work and during the nineteenth and early twentieth century proliferated in Coventry. Few survived, except the major national unions.

VAUXHALL

At the junction of Holbrook Lane and Foleshill Road was once a small area known as Vauxhall. Here stood a large house known as Vauxhall House which later had a front yard paved with overturned gravestones. It is possible that a small pleasure ground stood here in the eighteenth century which was named after London's famed Vauxhall Gardens. Although all references to the original Vauxhall have now disappeared, surprisingly the name can still be seen prominently displayed at a Vauxhall car dealership here.

WATCH MAKING

One of the first references to the watch trade in Coventry was in 1727 when George Porter, Coventry's mayor, was described as a watchmaker. By the middle of the century watch making was firmly established in the city, together with clock making which had begun in the previous century. Samuel Vale started watch production in 1747 and later became Vale, Howlett & Carr. Vale was to become the business partner of Richard Rotherham. Some Coventry watchmakers had considerable reputations, such as a Mr Arnold who in 1764 demonstrated before King George III a repeating watch so small it would fit into a ring. Other well-known makers of the time were Thomas Heath, Thomas Hales and Henry Harding. Larger manufacturers include Vale & Howlett, Bradshaw & Ryley, Mann & Wall and Carr & Rotherham to

*Coventry watches
made in 1898.*

name a few. Outside the factory system many individual watchmakers worked from home, each working on a different part of the watch. Watch making areas grew around the city, based in the Butts, Spon End, Chapelfields and Earlsdon. Earlsdon and Chapelfields themselves were particularly important areas which had largely been built to take the growing watch making population. Many smaller manufactories could also be found here, such as John Player, a notable watchmaker in Bedford Street.

Coventry had become one of the most important centres for the production of hand-made gold and silver pocket watches. In 1841 there were 473 men and 130 apprentices in the trade. By 1860 there were 90 watch manufacturers in the city employing 1,340 men, 667 apprentices and 30 women. Many of these watches carried rough movements made in Prescot in Lancashire. In that same year watch making and weaving were both badly hit by the Free Trade Act. Up until the creation of this Act many Coventry-made watches were exported to America, but the new Act put an 80 per cent tariff on the watches, hitting trade hard. During 1860 99,000 mass-produced American watches were imported into England and in 1861 this had risen to a flood of 160,000, an increase of 60 per cent, which meant fewer and fewer hand-made Coventry watches were sold. Many were driven out of the trade and, according to watch manufacturer Kevitt Rotherham, many left the watch making trade and went on to work in the new cycle factories.

In 1870–1, after a temporary boom due to the Franco-German War, the trade went into decline owing to the continual flow of cheap American and Swiss watches. The trade continued with rises and slumps but never got back to how it had been. By 1911 the number employed in the trade had dropped to 1,429. Production continued in the city but only on a small scale with companies such as Rotherham's and Coventry Movement. Many watchmakers survived by repairing watches and diversifying.

WATER SUPPLY

The site of Coventry had many natural sources of water, including the Bablake and its later surviving fragments such as the Mill Dam, St Osburg's Pool and the Swanswell Pools (there were originally two). The Sherbourne and Radford Brook and River Albert also gave a constant supply of water. There were, however, dozens of natural springs within the confines of the city, some around the bottom of Broadgate Hill such as St Agnes's Well, giving exceptionally pure drinking water, and some at the top of the hill.

It is thought one of the earliest recorded wells in the city was the Broad Well which still lies buried underground between the Old Grammar School and the AXA-Equity and Law building, at the entrance to Well Street. It had been suggested that the well was constructed in 1333 but it is generally now agreed to be much older. In the nineteenth century several people drowned in the well and it was covered over. Jordan's Well, which still lies under the road outside what was the old Gaumont Cinema, now the Dame Ellen Terry Building, was believed to have been constructed in 1349 at the expense of Coventry mayor Jordan Sheppey. It is however now known that the well itself was in existence before Sheppey was born.

The actual siting of Coventry's great monastery of St Mary was no doubt due to the availably of water from the top of Broadgate Hill. There are at least three wells and a spring in and around St Mary's Hall, the old castle site, and in the seventeenth century a small watercourse was noted as passing through Holy Trinity church and running down the hill. This watersource, probably

St Catherine's Well photographed when it stood in the Conduit Meadows. The well now stands between houses in Beaumont Crescent, Coundon.

spring-fed from the hill top, would naturally flow down through the site where it could be manipulated to supply cooking, washing and toilet facilities and then drain off through the stone-lined drain and a log pipe into the river below.

Coventry Priory itself owned one watersource which stood on its land, notably St Catherine's Well (now in Beaumont Crescent, Coundon), also known as Conduit Knob, which in the late fifteenth century had a stone chapel-like structure built over it. Pipes were used from this to supply conduits in the ancient Spon area of the city and the bottom of Smithford Street. The fact that this spring was dedicated to St Catherine suggests it was of an older origin, having pre-Christian connection. The spring also has a story attached to it about an underground tunnel, typical to ancient pre-Christian wells.

It wasn't until 1632 until any major change was made to part of the water supply when Bewley and Sargeson constructed the Swanswell Water Works which by pressure filled a reservoir in Cuckoo Lane. This was one of the city's main supplies apart from the waterworks in Spon End which in 1819 was leased by the corporation to Samuel Vale, a glazier. He leased the site for seven years on condition that he kept in repair all the walls, pipes, reservoirs and all other articles, 'connected with the works or spring of water . . . to supply the two usual conduits in Spon Street with water'. Due to the availability of natural springs in the area a new water works was opened in Spon End in 1847.

☛ *See* SWANSWELL POOL

WATSON, SAMUEL

Perhaps Coventry's most famous clockmaker was Samuel Watson, patronized by none other than Issac Newton. Watson was mathematician in ordinary to King Charles II and made a number of clocks for the King. Watson clocks were unusual in that they also showed the motions of the planets, the first to do so for 300 years. In 1695 Watson made a bracket clock which, apart from telling the time, showed the day and month, the stars overhead, the position of the sun, phases of the moon and the high tide. It also predicted eclipses. This clock is thought to have been made for Newton himself for he certainly owned it. Watson made an astronomical clock for King Charles who unfortunately died before its completion. The clock which represented the motions of the planets and zodiac was eventually purchased by Queen Mary for the vast sum of £1,000. The clock is now in the library at Windsor Castle.

☛ *See* WATCH MAKING

WEAVING

By the fourteenth century Coventry was one of the top centres in the Midlands for the wool trade. Apart from the sale of wool, mainly from the Wool Hall in Bayley Lane, there was a thriving weaving trade. The finished cloth was sold from the Drapery next to the Wool Hall in Bayley Lane. From the fifteenth century to the end of the sixteenth century much of this cloth was dyed blue with 'Coventry true blue'. The dye's lasting fastness made it noted throughout England. It was created by using woad mixed with madder and sloe berries. Coventry True Blue became so noted it appeared in numerous poems and rhymes. Production of this cloth made Coventry the fourth richest town in England. By the sixteenth century Coventry cloth and True Blue were being faked. To combat this all Coventry-woven cloth was first sent to the Searching House next to the Wool Hall. Here the quality of the weaving was checked by two weavers and fullers especially appointed for the task. If it met the approved standards a lead seal bearing the elephant and castle would be attached to the bale. So by the seal, 'men schall perceive and see it is true Coventry cloth'.

The beginning of the eighteenth century saw the decline of the wool trade, which was replaced by other trades such as the weaving of worsted cloth and the beginning of the silk ribbon weaving trade. In 1705 mayor William Bird set up a silk ribbon weaving works, possibly with the help of Huguenots skilled in the trade. By 1756 Bird employed some 2,000 handloom weavers. Other works sprang up and Coventry became the centre of the ribbon weaving in the Midlands. The early ribbons woven in Coventry were all black but later a rainbow of colours poured forth from Coventry looms. By 1782 Coventry was the home to 10,000 ribbon weavers. In 1820 the Jacquard loom was introduced to the city, leading to a great improvement in the intricacies of design of the patterns on ribbons. Many weavers worked from home and weaving districts developed around the city around Foleshill and Hillfields. Others worked in the small ribbon works scattered around the city. The introduction of steam-powered looms into the city led to a riot and the destruction of Josiah Beck's factory. It was another five years before anyone else dared to try to introduce the steam loom. By 1857 there were 25,000 weavers in Coventry and its suburbs, while 2,500 of them worked steam looms. In 1859 disruption hit the trade when the weavers demanded to be paid piecework and not by the fixed rate; a lockout began which lasted for eight weeks. Through council intervention and the threats of the mob the weavers won and got their piecework. All was well until 1860 when the government introduced the Free Trade Act which allowed cheap French ribbons to be imported with no duty. The market was flooded and the following year America put a massive import duty on English ribbons. Employers tried to drop the weavers' wages and they went on strike. This led many of the weavers and their families to reach the brink of starvation. Soup kitchens were opened in St Mary's Hall and Browett's factory.

During this period many weavers left the city, moving into other areas or countries. The strike turned into a slump from which the weaving trade never recovered. Many who wished to return to work could not as it no longer existed. By the mid-1860s the worst was over and the reduced weaving trade produced different items such as worsted weaving and cotton spinning. Other looms were adapted to weave elastic web, coach lace and muslin frilling. Apart from a short revival in 1870, weaving was in continual decline. In 1890 ribbons once more fell from style and prices halved, leaving the trade on its knees. Few survived into the twentieth century except the more specialist

firms – such as the firm of Thomas Stevens who produced pictorial ribbons and pictures known as Stevengraphs which are still highly collectable today. Another survivor was J and J Cash who produced silk pictures and still do.
☛ *See* BECK RIOTS

WESLEY, JOHN

John Wesley, the father of the Methodist faith, visited Coventry on a number of occasions. In his journal under the dates of 21/22 July 1779 he wrote:

> *When I came to Coventry I found notice had been given for my preaching in the Park, but the heavy rain prevented. I sent to the Mayor (Edward Harper) desiring the use of the Town Hall [Guildhall]. He refused; but the same day gave the use of it to a dancing master. I then went to the Woman's market. Many soon gathered together, and listened with all seriousness. I preached there again the next morning and again in the evening. Then I took coach for London. I was nobly attended, behind the coach were ten convicted felons, loudly blaspheming and rattling their chains; by my side sat a man with a loaded blunderbuss and another upon the coach.*

Three years later on 15 July 1782 he writes:

> *I preached at nine in a large school room at Coventry, at the bottom of St Michael's Churchyard . . . the poor little flock at Coventry, have at length procured a neat convenient room in the Woman's Market, only it is far too small. As many of the people could get in were all attention. How is the scene changed here also! I know not but now the Corporation, if it had been proposed, would have given the use of the Town Hall to me rather than to the dancing master!*

Wesley's poor little flock continued to worship in the small room at the back of the open market square, then moved on to a room at Whitefriars, then acquired the old Baptist Meeting House in Jordan Well. From here they moved to a large room at New Court in Gosford Street before acquiring the chapel formerly used by the Calvinists. Then the group decided to erect their own chapel in Warwick Lane and during the time it was being built they worshipped in St Mary's Hall, which would have pleased Wesley. The first Wesleyan hall was opened on 3 April 1836.

WHITE, SIR THOMAS.

Sir Thomas White was born in Reading in 1492. He traded as a merchant tailor and was made mayor of London in 1553. White's mayoralty was during the period of Wyatt's rebellion and Thomas received a knighthood for closing the gates on London Bridge against the rebels. Sir Thomas became quite rich and put his money to good cause by founding St John's College, Oxford. He

Sir Thomas White's statue on Greyfriars Green.

endowed the college with fifty scholarships, including two for Coventry. He also made charitable benefactions to Bristol and Leicester. Coventry's most noted benefaction from White was known as the 'Four Pounds Gift'. White purchased various pieces of land and property and directed that the interest of one part of it should be given annually to twelve poor men in sums of £2 each as a 'free gift'. Then the interest of another part should be lent in sums of £10 to four 'young men of good name and thrift', who were freemen after having served as apprentices. Over the years as the values of the properties increased so did the gifts and loans. After the suppression of the guilds in 1547 the council used over £1,300 from Sir Thomas White to purchase the old guild and chantry lands, some of which were sold in 1848 to lay out Hales Street.

Things did not always run well for in 1711 it was discovered that the mayor and council had actually embezzled £2,000 from the charity. This resulted in the forced sale of all of the city's civic plate to repay the debt. Also the council faced the shame of losing their civic heart, St Mary's Hall, for six long years, when it was rented out to all-comers. The charity however continued to bring in the money and some young freemen received as much as £100 to set up businesses. By 1851 Sir Thomas White's Charity Estate had a surplus of £18,000. In 1883 a statue was set up on Greyfriars Green to commemorative Coventry's most notable benefactor and the money supplied by Sir Thomas still brings in an income today.

WHITEFRIARS

The Whitefriars or Carmelites founded their house in Coventry in 1343, assisted by Sir John Poultney. All Carmelite houses were dedicated to the Virgin Mary and all inmates wore white in her honour. These monks lived austere lives and were well liked by the people, which brought in many gifts and helped to sustain the house. The friary itself stood in ten acres of grounds and consisted of a large 303 foot central towered church and the main friary buildings, of which all that survive are the gateway in Much Park Street and the main cloister on the London Road.

One of the friary's main incomes came from the Shrine of Our Lady of Coventry, a statue set within a painted chamber in the city wall, standing near the cloisters on the London Road and New Gate. This shrine had become nationally famous and was on the main pilgrimage list. Its importance lay in the fact that it was believed to protect travellers and many resorted to it. It was the practice of those who passed the shrine daily to salute it, thus a nearby inn bore the name, The Salutation. The Whitefriars was one of the first houses in Coventry to be dissolved by the crown. The foundation had a yearly income of under £8 so the sale of the buildings proved to be the main

Whitefriars photographed just before the laying out of the ring road.

revenue. The warden and thirteen brothers of Whitefriars were evicted from the house with no pension and John Hales purchased the building for £83, turning it into his own private residence called Hales Place. He initially established a school within the church, which didn't actually belong to him. This church was shortly afterwards demolished, leaving only the central tower standing for a few years.

WHITEFRIARS GATE

Whitefriars or Much Park Street Gate is believed to have been built around 1352; it was not one of the city wall gates but the entrance to Whitefriars Friary and church. Originally taller, it had two statues set in niches over the gate arch, one possibly the Virgin and the other St Peter. The gate stands in Much Park Street, which was a main road into the city from London. The narrow cobbled lane the gateway spans became Whitefriars Lane after the Dissolution of the Monasteries in the sixteenth century, when the friary was surrendered to the King's commissioners.

Sir Ralph Sadler then acquired the gatehouse as part of the Whitefriars estate and sold it on to John Hales with the cloister, which Hales turned into a private house. When Queen Elizabeth I stayed at Hales Place she passed through this gate, as did Mary Queen of Scots and King James I in 1617. The Hales family owned the gate until the eighteenth century, then in 1801, when

Whitefriars Gate in 1890.

Whitefriars was converted into a workhouse, the gateway was altered from a single dwelling into two.

All the stage coaches from London drove past this gate as they entered the city. Charles Dickens is said to have used it in his novel, *The Old Curiosity Shop*. He wrote:

> *The moon was shining down on the old gateway of the town, leaving the low archway very black and dark; and with a mingled sensation of curiosity and fear, she [Little Nell] slowly approached the gate, and stood still to look up at it. There was an empty niche from which some old statue had fallen or been carried away hundreds of years ago . . . The street beyond was so narrow and the shadow of the houses on one side of the way so deep, that they seem to have risen out of the earth.*

During the nineteenth century the two dwellings within the gate were homes to coal dealers, weavers, butchers, wardrobe dealers and drapers. In 1901 a clothes and boot seller Zakeriah Peach used to line the windows with highly polished boots. When he died rumours circulated that he had hidden a hoard of money in the building, which led to the interior being stripped by all and sundry. They found nothing but left the building in a dangerous condition. In 1962 former councillor Ron Morgan leased the semi-derelict building from the council and restored it, setting up as a potter there. In 1973 Ron opened it to the public as a toy museum, displaying toys he had collected dating from 1740. After his recent death the future is uncertain.

WHITTLE, SIR FRANK

Frank Whittle was born in 1907 at 72 Newcombe Road, Earlsdon. As a young man he attended the local school and quickly acquired the nickname of 'Mr Brains'. Frank saw his first aeroplane one day when walking upon Hearsall Common. It was flying so low it blew his hat off into a gorse bush. This sparked his interest in flying and when he was old enough he joined the RAF where he quickly got tagged the 'crazy flyer'. It was in Coventry, while living in Regent Street in 1929, that Frank first conceived the idea of using a gas turbine to build a jet-propelled engine.

In 1937 he tested his first experimental jet engine at Rugby and on 15 May 1941 the first flight of a Gloster E28, powered by two of Frank's jet engines, took place: it reached speeds of up to 370 miles per hour. Three years later news of the first jet was released to the world. Frank, the son of an Earlsdon factory foreman, became Sir Frank Whittle in 1948 and was thereafter known as the 'Father of the Jet Engine' or the man who shrank the world. In the year 2000 the Whittle Arch was erected in Millennium Square to commemorate him and in June 2007 a bronze statue of Sir Frank was unveiled on the same spot.

WYKEN PIPPIN

Wyken Pippins were once the most common apples grown in the Coventry area, but only a handful of trees now survive. It is said that Admiral Thomas Craven, one of the Cravens of Coombe Abbey, brought a seedling back from Holland and planted in William Skelton's garden at Sergeant's Farm on the Hillfields/Wyken border around the year 1720. This tree, previously unknown in England, flourished in its new home and soon began to spread throughout the area, becoming the most favoured of all the pippin apples. The Wyken pippin was not only noted for its prolificness, sweetness and crispness but also its ability to keep and improve with time. Apples picked at the end of September were particularly good at Christmas and would still be palatable in late February.

X

X MARKS THE SPOT

In the mid-nineteenth century Coventry artist and antiquarian Dr Nathanial Troughton lived in Priory Row near Hill Top. One day while workmen were digging at the rear of his property they unearthed an early medieval stone coffin, possibly of one of the early bishops or priors of St Mary's. Unusually Troughton had the men leave the coffin in situ and afterwards, so no one would forget where it was, he painted a white 'X' above it on his garden wall.

Another thirteenth-century coffin found on the site of Timothy Whites (Wetherspoons) in 1937.

Y

YUGOSLAVIA

Belgrade and Sarajevo in Yugoslavia are both twinned with Coventry and in 1952 that country gave a large quantity of good-quality beech for Coventry's post-war reconstruction. Some of it was requested to be used for the interior of the Belgrade Theatre, named after that city. Another large quantity of beech was used in 1952 to make a copy of the timbered roof in St Mary's Hall, to replace the blitz-damaged original. The remaining wood was used in the construction of council houses.

Z

ZULU

During the 1960s, standing astride the entrance to Coventry Zoo in Whitley, was a giant 60 foot high fibre-glass figure of a Zulu warrior holding a shield and spear. Coventry Zoo, although small, had a varied collection of animals, including elephants, lions and a polar bear. The zoo closed in the early 1970s.